MW00452491

"An empowering beacon of hope for those navigating the tangled webs of dissatisfaction, *Hurdles in a Girdle—Holding Life Together When You're Bursting at the Seams* offers invaluable insights and practical guidance to women grappling with the suffocating constraints of a toxic marriage, career, or life in general. Through Allen's anecdotes and empowering strategies, this book serves as a lifeline, illuminating the path towards reclaiming one's genuine self and forging a brighter, more fulfilling future. A must-read for anyone seeking to break free from the confines of their circumstances and embrace the boundless possibilities that await beyond, revealing the true purpose of life."

—Jack Canfield, Co-author of the #1 *NY Times* Best-Seller *Chicken Soup for the Soul Series* and #1 *NY Times* Best-Seller, Success Principles.

"*Hurdles in a Girdle* takes you by the hand from page one and has you clapping at the end. Filled with love, life, and laughter . . . Hurdles in a Girdle is awe-inspiring, and a must read!"

—Patty Aubery, #1 *New York Times* Best-selling Author, *Chicken Soup for the Christian Soul*

"Allen's 'bare all' memoir about love, laughter, and loss is an inspiration to learn that it is never too late to conquer all! Pat takes you from 'pain to triumph,' and 'poverty to penthouse!' Great read!!"

—Rhonda Shear, Hollywood actress, comedian, author, intimate apparel creator and designer of the Ahh Bra

HURDLES
IN A
Girdle

HURDLES
IN A
Girdle

Holding Life Together
When You're Bursting
at the Seams

Pat Allen

Published by Morningstar Publishing

ISBN (paperback): 978-0-9723200-2-3
ISBN (ebook): 978-0-9723200-3-0

Book design and production by www.AuthorSuccess.com

Printed in the United States of America

To my two children, Lee and Julie, who managed to live through the hurdles, my dear mama, who inspired me without knowing it, and my sweet Pat who will remain the love of my life.

Contents

Foreword

Jumping hurdles in a girdle doesn't sound like fun . . . and it isn't! The journey towards a content and gratifying life is filled with challenges and obstacles that can leave us feeling trapped and thoroughly unhappy, akin to a firefly trapped in a jar with a tight lid. Initially, it emits brilliance, but soon it grapples to break free, only to find the tiny air holes insufficient for a flight to freedom.

In this book, I delve into the hurdles spanning every facet of my life, ranging in size from small to extra-large yet jump I did over each one. My goal is to instill inspiration in you, the reader, urging you to attain the confidence and latent strength necessary to lead a more fulfilling and joyful life; a life with purpose.

Perhaps you harbor thoughts that staying stuck is the easier route, or you believe you're too old, or a myriad of reasons dissuade you from leaping to the other side where opportunities await. Whether ensnared in a mundane marriage, entangled in an unfulfilling career, grappling with familial strife, codependent relationships, friendship betrayals, or a precarious spiritual journey—this is a compelling read for you.

This book adopts the age-old adage, "If I can do it, you can do it," resonating from the perspective of a humble country girl who contended with life's formidable obstacles and transformed into a successful businesswoman who sold her enterprise for a sum beyond her imagination. The journey, fraught with every conceivable impediment, was surmountable through determination and the ability to leap over high hurdles, ultimately leading to a life of contentment. This life is attainable for you as well; it's your time to shine and craft a great life beyond your wildest dreams.

Life, Death, and All the Rest

As the sands of time have sifted through my fingers and I've grappled with the loss of loved ones, contemplation about the purpose of life has become a frequent companion. Why do we exist? Surely, not merely to survive, deciphering life's options, and then witnessing our bodies succumb to deterioration. What lasting impact do we leave behind? Is there a genuine purpose to our existence? I finally found the answers, and by the end of this book, so will you.

March 22, 2022, marked a pivotal moment for me. Unbeknownst to me, a perforated bowel allowed E. coli to spread its poison throughout my body. The resulting abdominal pain led to an urgent ultrasound, an emergency room visit, a critical procedure, and a subsequent nine-day intravenous antibiotic treatment. Numerous doctors attested to my luck in being alive.

Facing this reality prompted reflections on my life and the potential legacy I might leave. Contemplating the chaos my daughter might encounter had I passed away during that time—papers scattered, an unmade bed, and clothes strewn about—I realized I might have been dead, but I would have been embarrassed!

Over the past year, I've pondered my life's impact on others, prompting me to document my experiences for those who wish to explore their own journey. From a barefoot country girl living on a dirt road to a lady in suits and high heels who successfully created a multi-million-dollar real estate firm, my journey was laden with hurdles—both triumphant and disheartening moments that paved the way for my success. I share these personal stories with moments of happiness, sadness, spirituality, and humor to inspire and motivate others to achieve their goals. You have the opportunity to trade your girdle that is squeezing life from you for big girl pants and then learn the happy dance! The choice is up to you.

CHAPTER 1

Poor Girl with Skinny Legs, a Snake, and the Goat Man

I think when you're a young child you just expect everyone to grow up the same way you did. My first memory is one in a country setting with a tire swing tied by thick rope in an old oak tree that brought giggles to a three-year-old. The yard was sparse of grass and the old gray house was of wood desperately in need of paint. Daylight was seen through the cracks and cold wind ensured the need for blankets and quilts. piled high on my little bed. Nearby was a creek with a small wooden bridge, and my brother and I would throw rocks and watch them skip across to find their final destination.

Up a winding dirt road was a large watermelon patch with vines of gold and green filled with plump melons of sweetness. My memory of us breaking into one by hitting it on the ground and eating it on the spot in the summer sun led me to like my watermelons warm rather than cold. Looking back, we couldn't afford a lot of food, and melons and tomatoes in the fields were delicacies.

I remember coming home one night to our house that was in total darkness. When Mama turned on the light, everyone started screaming as a snake embedded itself into the sofa cushion! To this day, I am terrified of any and all snakes due to the hysteria this event caused in my early years! They say there are "good snakes" and "bad snakes," but I say a snake is a snake and run no matter which way it slithers!! It's a southern "thang" to always turn off lights when you leave a room or leave home for the evening, but not for me because of snake phobia!

When I was three years old, we moved to a house in a different area, but still in the country and located down a dirt road. Trees lined the other side of the road, and I was a bit of a tomboy and liked to climb them! Mama and Daddy were so proud to have a new house because he built it with people he knew, not being able to afford a builder. Just a few things were lacking, and the major blunder was forgetting built-in-closets, so as an afterthought they had to be extended into the bedrooms, taking up even more space in the tiny bedroom I shared with my sister. There was little or no insulation, and no air conditioning, so looking back now I realize that I grew up in a sauna; the heat and humidity in Macon Georgia summers were unbearable! Maybe that contributed to me weighing only ninety-four pounds when I left for college, and I'm five feet, four inches tall!

We never had much money, and my dad was a binge drinker. Sometimes he would get paid on Friday and go out and spend the money on whisky that he downed before driving home. We would wait on him for dinner, and I remember praying he would come home sober and with a paycheck. Sometimes he did, sometimes he didn't. I could see the worry on Mama's face, as we were behind on bills many times. They would argue, but eventually she would forgive him . . . until the next time.

My mother was strong and independent. She drove a taxi during World War II and saved every penny to buy a car. She was born into poverty, and at three years old was "farmed out" to my great aunts and uncles in Florida, and when old enough to work in the fields she was made to do so. She was separated from her biological sister who was sent to Athens, Georgia, to work for another great aunt and uncle she came to dislike very much. They both were sent away to be used for child labor and never had a loving family. Money they "earned" would go to my grandmother to feed the younger kids. My grandmother was married three times, once to a Methodist preacher who died, and then to my mama's dad, who was so jealous he would rake the dirt in the yard when he left for work so he could see the footprints if anyone had come to the house. He disappeared before my mother was born, never to be seen again.

Mama was forced to drop out of school when she was in sixth grade because she was deemed old enough to work in the fields, picking fruit and sometimes cotton. She knew the pain of bleeding fingers from doing so. At some point, she came back to Macon to take care of the younger children and met my dad at a dance club and later they were married on Christmas Eve. His drinking would become an issue that added more sorrow to her life.

She had no role model as a mother and did the best she could. She was a waitress for years and after becoming a mother became a housewife. She was not a great cook, and I think I ate enough fat and cholesterol during those years that it caused the fatty liver I have today. Bacon grease filled the round silver metal container that sat on the stove, and everything was fried or filled with this grease! Fried chicken, fried pork chops, country-fried steak, fried okra, fried corn, fried squash, French fries, fried apple pies, hoe cakes, just to name a few . . . makes my liver quiver just thinking about it! Adjacent to the kitchen was a large Motorola stand-alone radio that played most of the day, and perhaps that is where my love of music took hold, and maybe hearing love songs brought her joy and hope of a better life.

My brother was ten years older than me and my sister five years older, so I sort of felt like I grew up alone. I do have fond memories of going fishing with my dad in his old Ford pick-up truck, with cane poles in the back with red corks waiting to bob and make it happen. Sometimes we would go to a small lake at a nearby dairy, and my dad was quite a jokester telling me chocolate milk came right out of brown cows!

I guess I should have known I would grow up "prissy," because I wouldn't put the squiggly worm on the hook or take the poor fish off; it would just lay flopping in the grass! My mama loved to fish also, so there are many good memories of our days together waiting to see who caught the biggest one! We would sit for hours on the grassy bank in the heat and humidity, but there was peace and serenity in that place, and we were together. Mama would eventually pull Vienna sausages, canned sardines, slices of onions, and saltines from brown paper bags and we fed ourselves while our worms fed the fish.

Another fond memory is the Goat Man, who was a hobo and icon to so many. He traveled in a large and rickety wooden wagon pulled by goats and sold postcards to make money for food for himself and the goats. I would get so excited when I would see him on the corner block! He had sparse and coarse gray hair and a long fuzzy beard that was well below his shoulders. I loved the goats, especially the little ones he was sometimes cradling in his thin arms. He had signs saying, "Jesus Saves" and was a good man. There were empty cans that were always clanging when he was on to a new destination. There was a sense of excitement in the air when he was in the area, and I considered him a celebrity! He traveled the southeast, and his history can be found on the internet. I have a drawing of him in my great room today and it brings me peace and good memories. The last thing I heard about him was he was on his way to California to find Morgan Fairchild and had an accident of some sort. He wound up in the same nursing home where sweet Minnie, my deaf-mute friend, died (more on that later in an upcoming chapter.) His life ended there also; rather interesting that two people who were an integral part of my life would share the same facility and pass away there, albeit at different times.

A sad note: I learned a few years ago that he was traveling in Tennessee and several thugs started harassing and throwing rocks at him. They then stole one of his favorite goats and barbequed it and brought it back for him to see. The hatred and cruelty of some people is pure evil. We now see this today with mass shootings. God help us all.

Childhood memories remind us that the best things in life are free, and no amount of money can replace the warm feelings of love they conjure up. You will never know the impact sweet memories linger with others when you've passed on.

CHAPTER 2

A Lesson and a Blessing: Never Keep the Quarter

A lesson from my dad when I was a little girl was profound, and I often wonder if he knew he was teaching me a lifelong lesson. On Sundays, we always dressed in our "finest" and attended a small Methodist church, and Daddy would give me a quarter and a dime that I put in my tiny change purse. The quarter was for the offering plate and the dime was for me to spend as I chose during the week. There was always a choice I could make, looking at the shiny coins knowing what I should do, and the few times I kept the quarter instead of the dime, I felt so guilty and worried about it all week! That was my first experience with temptation, and a few times the devil got me! I couldn't wait for next Sunday to give my quarter and make it right with God!

I was excited, as a little girl, to dress up for church in the few frilly dresses we could afford with lacy socks and little shoes that buckled. I even remember shining them with a biscuit, unaware that the lard was the polish; I thought it was some magic trick Mama knew! And at Easter, I always had a cute bonnet with a sash and little white gloves. Maybe my overfilled closet today and the way I dress reminds me of those days that were filled with God's love and us as a family, at least on Sundays.

After church, sometimes we would "window shop" on Cherry Street in downtown Macon, and I would long for the things I saw. I saw a dress once that I thought would look great on Mama. I asked her how much it was and said I wanted to buy it for her. She said, "I don't know, but there is no way we can afford it!" I replied, "Mama, one day I'll buy it for you!"

How could I have known that one day I could buy anything we saw in those windows? I could even buy her a house today if she were still living. I've often wondered how Mama afforded to dress us at all, not knowing until Friday afternoons until I saw Daddy's truck headed down our road if the paycheck was safe. Then all was right in my world, for another week, anyway.

If you must question whether you want children, you probably shouldn't have them. They deserve your undivided attention and love. They are God's greatest gift to us but are a full-time responsibility that doesn't end. If you are not happy with who you are that will pass on to children who will struggle and never be happy with themselves. Phones and video games can never take the place of parenting and have the ability to conjure up a cruel and dangerous cyberspace, leading to bullying and sometimes suicide. A phone can't take the place of reading bedtime stories, a sweet hug, a goodnight kiss, and the words: "I love you" before turning out the light.

When Mama died, I didn't just cry because she left this world, but for the sad life she was given through no fault of her own. Many people simply aren't given chances in life. You never know the impact you have on another. Everyone is struggling in their own way ... reach out and be a light in someone else's darkness. Kindness is contagious and doesn't cost a dime ... or a quarter.

CHAPTER 3

Pigs, Chickens, and a Childhood Friend

As a little country girl, we played in the yard until dark or until mama would yell "WHOOHOO!" That was our signal that dinner was ready. We played dodgeball and a game of kick the cans, where everyone only had time to hide until the "it" person stacked them again. I used to walk in the woods across from our house, and I think it must be national forest land because it hasn't been built on to this day. I would climb trees and was a little tomboy for a while and felt I could do anything the boys could do and went on the prove it later in life!

The house next door belonged to my Uncle Edwin, but he had a falling out with my dad when I was little, so I was forbidden to go there. But my cousins and I would play outside and hide if we saw their dad's truck approaching. He was mean and an alcoholic. My aunt was so sweet, but back then women couldn't get out of bad situations due to lack of money and nowhere to go. I always felt sorry for her and knew what a hard life she was living.

We had a fenced backyard and always had animals. I had two pigs that I named, played with, and spent time with. They were my smart pets and would run to me when I went outside. I would treat them as if they were my dogs and I loved them. When the day came to kill them for food, I was traumatized and refused to eat any part of them. To this day, I can recall the smell of chitterlings! I cried for days but had to realize we needed food. We also had chickens and roosters. They were mean and would come run up at times and spur my legs if I didn't outrun them! That's when I became a runner ... LOL!

My grandmother also had chickens, and on Sundays the entire family on my mother's side would meet for lunch after church and it was always quite a spread. The kitchen was large with tables pushed together, a vinyl tablecloth, and chairs pulled from every room in the house. There was not enough room for everyone to be seated at the same time, so children had to eat last! There were casseroles, fried corn, pole beans, johnny cakes, potato salad (my mama made the best!), coleslaw, cakes, banana pudding (that's my favorite to this day), and of course the real "free-range chicken" that had roamed my grandmother's yard only a few hours before! Several times, I watched my grandmother wring a chicken's neck and it flopped the around the pen until it died and wound up on a platter before us. Again, traumatic, and I wouldn't eat it! Many years later, she passed away from an aneurysm while feeding her chickens and I watched as the ambulance carried her away. I was eighteen years old.

A memory comes to mind of the white clapboard house that was always too hot or too cold and always in need of paint. The neighbors on the corner were Black, and a classy couple. He was a postman, and several times I was invited into their home to visit and was envious of how nice it was. They also wore nice clothes and drove a nice car. I loved seeing pictures of their family, and knew they wanted the same things in life White people did. They were rich in my eyes in more ways than one.

A neighbor across the street from my childhood home had a big house with a circular driveway and they were wealthy in my eyes. The large yard was laden with large magnolia trees, and I loved watching the tight white buds loosen to beautiful petals and a scent that will always remind me of childhood. The girl who lived in that house was named Alice, and we became best friends. She was adopted, and I learned that her adopted dad had died suddenly so she was being raised by her adopted mom and grandmother. They had a large kitchen with nice countertops and wall to wall carpet in the other rooms. It was a mansion in my young eyes. The food was great, and they even had a maid to clean for them! I loved spending the night, knowing I would probably have warm cinnamon rolls for breakfast.

Alice and I remained friends throughout our teenage years, and she even got a car at sixteen! It was a Karmen Ghia and we loved to go for rides and spy on wannabe boyfriends. One night, we were out joyriding and got stuck in a ditch, and the guy we were scoping out had to come and help us. We were so embarrassed! We had many crazy adventures, as teenagers do. Alice and I basically lost touch as we went to different colleges, but those memories are still precious to me.

Many years later, after I married, the downtown bank I used had a drive-thru, and the teller reminded me so much of Alice. One day, I told her she reminded me of my childhood friend who by the way she looked and talked like. I told her they should meet, and when I told her Alice's name, she shocked me by responding, "She's my sister and we've been looking for her!"

I immediately called Alice and arranged the meeting. She learned that her biological parents lived in Macon and had an agreement that they would never contact Alice until her adopted mother had died. They had been in touch all those years and knew all about Alice's life, and after her adopted mother's death finally connected with her!

This was perhaps my first experience of connecting people, and God gave me the opportunity to help my friend meet her birth parents and family. It was rather remarkable!

CHAPTER 4

Big George and Little Me

As a young girl growing up in the country in Macon, Georgia, there is a memory that has stayed with me throughout the years. During the 1960s, the division between Whites and Blacks was an accepted reality. I vividly recall, as a little girl, an image of a large Black man standing at our back screen door which led to the kitchen. Our small house, covered in asbestos siding, had a tiny kitchen with a linoleum floor, a gas stove, no dishwasher except for my sister and me, and a metal table for four with a red Formica top and chrome legs. A white metal cabinet held our mismatched dishes.

One summer morning, I heard a knock on the back door, which required climbing a set of stairs to reach. My mother also heard it, and together we went to see who was there. It was Big George, a Black man wearing worn-out clothes but sporting a half-smile. My mother recognized him and asked, "Big George, what are you doing here?"

He replied, "I'm here to help Mr. Bill with some work around the house."

I can still hear my mother's response, "I know, but why are you at my BACK door? Come to the FRONT door, and I'll let you in!"

Those words spoken by my mother left a profound impact on me and spoke volumes about my parents' character. They believed that Black people were just as deserving as White people to enter through the front door. I watched as Big George nodded appreciatively and said, "Thank you, ma'am!"

It reminded me of the lessons from *To Kill a Mockingbird*, that this treatment didn't seem right. Curiosity got the better of me, and I asked my mother, "Why can't Black people always come to the front door like us?" Her reply was, "That's just the way it is, baby." Deep down, I felt that it had to change someday.

Many years later, when I read the book *The Help*, it brought back memories of a time when Black individuals were seen as inferior and limited to working for White people. They were barred from white establishments, and if they tried to sit at a downtown lunch counter, like at Woolworths in Macon, they were told to leave or faced arrest. I couldn't comprehend it, and it saddened me.

After graduating from medical technology school, I began working in a doctor's office in Macon when I was twenty years old. During orientation, as I was shown around, I discovered two separate waiting rooms and bathrooms with signs that read "Colored Only." It deeply troubled me, but challenging the status quo seemed daunting. Big George came to my mind immediately, and I wondered how his family was doing.

In the office, I got to know the two Black assistants, delightful young women who simply wanted a better life for their children. We became good friends and shared our daily stories, sitting outside and enjoying the lunches we brown-bagged. We couldn't be seen eating together in the breakroom. I would take their shift on my day off if one of their children was sick or they needed to go to the doctor to help them out.

I held onto the hope that Martin Luther King Jr. could bring about peaceful change in the face of discrimination, so his assassination hit me hard. The riots and the «us against them» mentality continued, fueled by hatred and senseless killings. I was both outraged and saddened that our country had reached such a state. I couldn›t understand why we couldn›t be as accepting as my mother was when I was a little white girl, talking to Big George in the yard, where we exchanged kindness. I even learned the names of his small children and I asked him once, "Big George, why don't you bring your kids over here to play one day?" He was quick to respond, "Oh, the neighbors wouldn't like that!" I was disappointed. His goals were no different from my father's: to earn enough to feed and clothe his children and teach them right from wrong.

*I learned early in life that a person's worth is not defined by their skin color but by the contents of their heart, and all hearts are red. We have made so much progress and I feel opportunities are there for all. There is a division that still does exist and has been accelerated by the media. Most people are accepting of others, as it should be. Be kind and teach your children to be color blind.

CHAPTER 5

Love on the Rocks and Hay Bales

I met a boy at a church function when I was fifteen. I was on a hayride with someone else who wouldn't keep his hands off me, so I made it clear I wanted to be left alone! The other guy and I had mutual friends and he had asked about me. We started dating, and this was my first experience trying to figure out relationships and love. He was sixteen, and we dated for two years until he left for college. I started to sense things weren't quite the same, but we saw each other as often as we could. I was so naïve, thinking this was real love and we would be married.

After one of our many breakups we had in high school, I was going to have a date with a cute guy I had met at a party. When my boyfriend heard of it, he started a fight with the other guy at school. When I was made aware of it, I was embarrassed to be part of such a thing. Our date was to be on Saturday night, but on Friday the new guy drowned in a swimming accident. I was shocked and sad, and his parents blamed me for putting a bad mark on his good name.

My boyfriend's parents forbade us to see each other after that, but we did sneak around. We kept the relationship going, and when I went to a different college, I was asked out by some really nice and handsome guys. I refrained, telling them I had a boyfriend. Little did I know he was seeing his mother's hairdresser in Macon. I saw them once sitting in the car together, too close for my comfort, and we ended it.

The pain of my first heartbreak was so real and I questioned why he chose her over me. I wondered what was wrong with me, and I was really depressed for a long time. I look back today and realize I gave him power over me and thought he could "fix" my insecurities. I now know I had to do that for myself—which I eventually did. My friends kept me going until I met someone else, even though he wasn't right either, so two wrongs didn't make Mr. Right!

Over the years, I have asked myself, "what is love?" What attracts different people and why does the pain cut so deep if it doesn't work? Why can't you just move on without carrying the heartache for years? Love is such a crucial need for every living being. Think of the mourning doves who mate for life, and mourn for life, with the one left watching over the deceased one with a fervent coo.

I still remember that when my kids were small, a neighborhood dog got his collar caught in a fence and choked to death. The other dogs gathered in silence, tails down, and one had tears rolling down his cheeks. I've heard that elephants gather and mourn when one dies. These are acts of love, but what is love between two people? Is there a need in us the other one fills, that is dormant until then? Do they bring out a joy we haven't felt? Do they make us laugh a lot, releasing dopamine? Do they make us a better person, who learns to like ourselves more? That is a huge responsibility to put on anyone!

To find love there needs to be a physical attraction, but that can be confused with lust. I had a lot of insecurities and thought my boyfriend could "fix" those for me. That is something to look out for, because one person can confuse the two and the other one gets hurt when the phone doesn't ring anymore, and excuses become too frequent. I think the "best friend theory" is a good one. Get to know differences and similarities and see if you are compatible. If you make each other laugh that is a good sign. If you don't, maybe rethink the connection.

The most important thing I know is you must learn to love yourself FIRST before you can really love someone else. If not, you will resent them for not being able to do that for you, and that responsibility should never be theirs. There is a 100 percent chance of divorce in that marriage, and I learned that to be true in my two years of therapy during my first marriage. I didn't know who I was or how to be a wife or mother at such an early age, and there are no classes on that subject taught in school.

CHAPTER 6

Beer Breath and Being Methodist

My high school years were when I realized that if your dad wasn't a professional, you weren't worthy of friendships with girls whose dads were. I went to an all-girls school of about 300 students in Macon, and though I was accepted in grammar school, it was because we all lived in the same district of lower income families. In high school, they came from surrounding areas, with the affluent rising to the top. I used humor to survive those years and never had the clothes or expensive shoes or fad purses that they did. I remember walking the halls between classes, and if one of the "chosen" girls spoke to me it made my day! How foolish, looking back, that teenagers feel that way and the impact that behavior of others has on your insecurities. Even though we didn't have bullies, the results were the same.

I went to parties and never drank (I'm a devout Methodist after all ... LOL) so I was the designated driver. To have an intoxicated teenager over-loaded with beer try to kiss me was disgusting. To this day I hate beer breath! I often wonder how many of them drank to hide the pain of being teenagers and how many just were out for fun with hormones raging. Either way, I wanted no part of it.

The scary thing is, I would have run off and married Mr. Wrong #1. I'm so very glad I didn't because a divorce would have been imminent. When I look at the life I've lived and the life he has lived, there is no comparison. To take on the role of June Cleaver was not in my playbook!

I think my high school experience of feeling inferior taught me to accept everyone. I appreciate people from all walks of life. I care as much for my blue-collar friends as I do for my affluent friends; good people are genuine whether they clean my house or are the CEO of a company. A good heart and a kind soul cannot be bought.

CHAPTER 7

Being Gay is Not Gay . . . Big Girls Do Cry

When I was fifteen years old, I was at a party in a rather large facility with high school friends and others who were invited, many of whom I had not met. There was a band and I'll always remember the song playing: "Go Away Little Girl." that may have been an omen, because my life would change forever that night. Beer was flowing and I was determined to be the "good girl" and not drink until age twenty-one; after all, I was a Methodist! I was talking to some friends when an attractive blond guy with beer breath approached us. He introduced himself, and when he heard my name said, "You're not related to (my brother's name), are you?"

When I said I was, he proceeded to tell me, in front of my friends, "He's a queer and just tried to pick me up!"

We were all stunned and silent as he wandered off, not knowing the pain I was feeling and would feel forever. My friends and I moved on to another discussion and didn't speak of this revelation again until many years later. When I went to bed that night, I cried myself to sleep.

I wasn't embarrassed as much as I was sad for Tom, knowing the hatred people had for gays in those years, this being 1964. I held it inside and remember an incident when we were in Athens, Georgia, visiting my aunt when Tom showed up with a black eye and bruised face. It scared me to see that, and his excuse was something meager like walking into a door. I could see whispers among the adults, and I knew he had been beaten for being gay.

He was ten years older than I, so I wasn't privy to adult conversations, I just knew something was wrong. As soon as he graduated from high school, Tom enlisted in the Navy. He was very handsome, with deep blue eyes and blonde hair. He had a Ford Fairlane convertible with a top that automatically folded down, and when he picked me up from grammar school, I felt like a princess! He was very smart, had a photographic memory, and went on to achieve a master's degree in history from Oglethorpe University.

When Tom came home from his four-year stint in the Navy he was living at home and attending Mercer University. Our house was tiny, and Tom had one of the first stereos, so any time music played we all heard it, even behind closed doors. I think this is where my love for Johnny Mathis music came from and I love it to this day!

I came home from school one day and Mama was crying. I'm sure she cried many times but concealed it. All I was told was that Tom was moving out. I would learn later that my dad had picked up the extension phone and heard Tom talking to a male lover. Since homosexuality, in my dad's eyes, was a mortal sin, he told Tom he had to leave his home.

I cried when he moved out and had a scar on my heart that would never heal. This had a profound effect on my life, because I knew what a great guy my brother was and felt that religion condemned him for something he was born with. An empathy grew inside me toward gays of all genders and ages. I have the most wonderful gay friends and it saddens me that they must be categorized as different. They have the same hearts as anyone else and share love like anyone else and have compassion like anyone else.

Mama never forgave my dad for that, and the tension would last until he died at age sixty-six. Tom moved to Atlanta into an older neighborhood, Little Five Points, where gays frequented. He took a job at General Motors after completing his master's degree and had a good management position. Once affirmative action was implemented, he was demoted, and when someone without experience took his position, he quit. This was another form of discrimination that forced him out once more into a new life.

At that point, Tom had bought a personal home and two rental houses in his neighborhood that was filled with older folks. They were craftsman-style with large front porches adorned with hanging ferns and bright red geraniums. One widowed lady and one "old maid" both had little, or no family and Tom befriended them, cutting their grass, buying their groceries, and taking them to doctor's appointments. He had a heart of gold and was a giver, expecting nothing in return.

One of the ladies was Miss Alice, as I called her. She had been a nurse in the day when women weren't allowed to achieve a career and was in her eighties. She was diminutive in size; her hair was snow white and always in a bun, and the contrast made her teeth take on a yellow tone. She had no family and became part of ours, spending holidays in Macon with us. She and Tom became inseparable, and anywhere he went she went. They even traveled to Greece together, with thoughts of moving there. When Miss Alice died, Tom was heartbroken and surprised to learn that she had left him her house! His inventory increased, and eventually he had five homes, four of which were rentals.

Tom was also an animal lover and took in strays, paying for their shots and neutering along with the large vet bills. He couldn't have them all in Atlanta, so he stayed most of the time in Macon at our childhood home that had a large, fenced yard. Both of our parents had passed away, and Tom had kept the house. It seemed that he was on a mission to help abused animals and would do so until the day he died. When he became ill, he told me and my daughter Julie to never clean out the bed of his old truck because there were two little mice who had babies and they were living there! Julie snapped a picture of the little creatures, who were no larger than my little finger.

On one of his quests, Tom had been watching a large dog in a poor neighborhood that was chained to a tree without water or food. After several days, he took wire cutters and cut the chain, and picked up the dog. As he ran to the car BBs flew by his head!

On another occasion, Tom was in a cemetery where he had been watching a pregnant dog that had taken up there. He would take the pregnant dog food and water, waiting for the puppies to arrive so he could care for them. He called me to ask if I knew a lady, with the last name Fickling, whom he had met by chance in the cemetery. I told him it was a prominent family name and later realized her sister-in-law owned a condo below mine in Highlands.

Kerri Fickling had also become a rescuer, and they were both watching the same pregnant mama. As it turned out, Kerri has a non-profit rescue organization, SOS Rescues, whose goal is to save stray dogs. She has a source up north where she transported those that weren't immediately adopted. She and Tom connected and saved many animals over the years. After his death, she posted a very nice tribute to Tom on Facebook, who she had felt was poor, but spent money to feed and rescue animals. I replied that he was educated, with a master's degree and owned four rental homes, and wasn't poor. Money was never important to him, and I think the pain of being hated for being gay led him to help eliminate pain in people and animals in any way he could.

I'm still sad that Tom faced such hatred in the name of religion when he was a better soul than many I know who sit in church on Sunday, not always for the right reason. I'm sad he never had a partner to adore him for the kind person he was who never hurt a soul. I'm sad he and my dad never really mended their relationship. I'm sad that Mama hurt so much seeing her son belittled and beaten, both mentally and physically, not unlike how Mary must have felt about Jesus.

*I've learned from two different generations, my brother, and my son, how discrimination hurts just because your sexual preference is different from the majority. This is not a choice one makes but one that is determined at birth. There is a hereditary component in most families with gay children. Why judge good people? Why single them out as targets who are taught to fight not by lesson but as a survival necessity? My brother was a great example of someone with a good heart who made a difference in the world, and that is all that matters. From first learning of him being gay when I was fifteen years old and being shocked and saddened by that news, as an adult I have witnessed the pain of my gay friends from all walks of life and all ages. We are only as strong as wrongs we right from the mistakes we experience. Be kind to all people and all of God's critters. They were created with love to give love. Hate and love are both four letter words . . . which do you choose for yourself?

UPDATE: This is a letter to the editor in response to a Baptist minister's column in Highlands written September 2023 who indicated that God hates gays. I couldn't remain silent and received many texts, emails, phone calls, and face to face acknowledgments thanking me for speaking out. My reply is always the same: "We ALL need to speak out."

Hate and Love are Both Four Letter Words

I am deeply saddened by the need to respond to Pastor Mark Ford's column on September 14 in our local newspaper. I had hoped that we had moved beyond the hurtful rhetoric against the LGBTQ+ community, and it is disheartening to find that a Baptist minister in Highlands, North Carolina felt compelled to engage in such discourse. My personal connection to this issue runs deep. When I was 15 years old, I learned by accident that my brother was gay. My father's reaction was to tell him to leave his house because he was a homosexual. My mother's heart shattered, and their marriage was never the same.

My brother faced physical violence from heterosexual individuals and even lost a job due to his identity. Despite all this adversity, he exhibited a level of kindness and compassion that surpassed anyone I knew. He made it his mission to provide shelter not only to stray animals but also to people in need. Even during the last Thanksgiving of his life, while battling pain and liver disease, he cooked a meal for a homeless man living under a bridge in Macon, Georgia. Despite his intelligence, a master's degree, and being financially secure, what truly mattered to him was helping those in need. After his passing, a woman shared how he had generously provided her and her daughter with free rent when they would otherwise have been homeless in Atlanta. When he passed away, our wonderful Humane Society took in the dogs and cats he had cared for, and I personally funded the painting of three of his dogs on their van in his memory and honor.

I also have a gay son, and I became aware of his sexual orientation when he was just 5 years old.

His likes and dislikes of sports and other activities revealed clues. Even though his generation experienced greater acceptance, he struggled with it, ultimately turning to alcohol as a coping mechanism as a teenager. He later gave up drinking, but the societal hatred he faced as a gay individual was a harsh burden. He went on to earn a PHD in philosophy. No one should have to hide their true self, especially when they have never harmed anyone.

One crucial fact missing from all these discussions, including the hate-filled letters to the Playhouse Board and others in town, as well as the Baptist minister's comments, is that individuals who identify as gay or lesbian are born this way. Mothers often have an innate understanding, and there appears to be a genetic predisposition within families. It is unfathomable to me that anyone would believe that these loving and compassionate individuals wake up one day and choose to be attracted to the same sex, knowing the hatred and discrimination they will face. Look at the gay individuals you know and ask yourself if you truly believe they made this choice.

They are inherently good-hearted and sensitive people who deserve the same opportunities as you and me. They do not choose their sexual orientation, and the high suicide rate among them is a stark reminder of the harm caused by societal prejudice. My gay friends are Christians. It pains me that a pastor would resort to such rhetoric, for God is love, and it seems that this sentiment is not always reflected in our actions. This reaffirms my pride in being a Methodist, who loves all and doesn't judge.

END OF LETTER.

CHAPTER 8

Marriage and Mistakes ...
Don't Eat the Hashbrowns!

I was nineteen when I married in July of 1967, and turned twenty that November. I had broken up with a boyfriend who two-timed me, and I was hurt and questioning if anyone could really love me. I had left college to attend a two-year program at the Macon Hospital School of Medical Technology, not because I was really interested in it, but because a lady I knew from church recommended it. It was quicker than staying in college for four years. I was homesick at college and decided to enroll.

We worked twenty-four-hour Sundays and came back at 5 p.m. until 7 a.m. on Monday morning. This went on for a week, and then our hours were either 7am--3pm or 3pm-11pm for two weeks. It was exhausting, and we had books to study and tests to take. The hospital had an emergency room, and we were constantly in demand for blood work on gunshot victims who needed blood immediately, and we had to crossmatch to be sure of a compatible blood type, or car wreck injuries, or any accident you can imagine. We developed a lot of strength and stamina we didn't know we had!

On weekends, friends gathered at a favorite restaurant where people sat in their cars and carhops in white coats came out to take your order. It was called "The Pig 'n Whistle" and all the young people went there in the evenings; girls looking for guys and guys looking for girls . . . like *Happy Days* on TV. I would learn later that "The Pig" employed Otis Redding, James Brown, Little Richard at various times and fed a myriad of celebrities including Cher, Elvis, Eric Clapton, Lynyrd Skynyrd, and the Allman Brothers. Guys occasionally trolled on foot while we girls sat there trying to fake it and look uninterested! My friend, Cheryl (who I adore to this day), and I were regulars, and we were always talking to people in various cars. Windows were down no matter how hot or cold it was, and rock and roll music was blaring.

One night, a tall, sandy-haired guy walked up to me and said, "I think you know my sister."

We had seen him a few times, but never had a conversation. I found him to be cute and he drove a Mustang, so my interest was increasing by the minute! I knew from his sister they lived in a nice neighborhood. We proceeded to talk, and he asked me out on a date. I was excited to go but would be embarrassed for him to see the little white asbestos shingled house where I lived, but there was nothing I could do about that.

He picked me up at home and was gracious and a gentleman, and it seemed we always went to his family's home for dinner. I remember having tapioca pudding for the first time and it was warm . . . I was in heaven! Fast food restaurants were just beginning, but we never went out to eat. I didn't think much about it at the time. He was a student at the University of Georgia (I remain an obnoxious bulldog fan to this day . . . Go DAWGS) so we saw each other on weekends. I was enrolled in medical technology school and my hours were hectic. The only car I could afford was one my dad found for $300; a Fiat that looked like a white box and soon refused to go in reverse. I had to always park on a hill so it could roll forward!

We dated about a year before Lee asked me to marry him. I was nineteen years old, and he was twenty-two. I was thrilled and scared at the same time. I knew his parents never thought I was good enough since I came from the wrong side of the tracks, but they knew he loved me. We had a small wedding in the chapel at Mulberry Methodist Church in Macon, with only our parents and siblings attending. He explained it by saying he didn't like crowds. This should have been a red flag, but I let it wave on.

We went To Saint Simons Island in Georgia for our honeymoon, and instead of staying at the renowned King and Prince Hotel, we stayed in a small motel he and his buddies always stayed in during spring break. We never went out for a meal but had to get takeout. Another red flag kept waving that I continued to ignore. I was miserable and told my best friend three weeks later that I thought I had made a mistake getting married.

When we returned home, we lived with his parents for several reasons. We couldn't afford an apartment since he was still in college, and I was still a student in lab training. Also, the draft was still mandatory in the '60s. Lee received a notice that he was being drafted and we knew the odds were he would be sent to Vietnam, as most were back then. We were both so upset, and Lee enrolled in the Navy Reserves to avoid the draft. He was ordered to attend Officer Candidates' School in the Great Lakes for three months and we had only been married three weeks.

It was obvious that his parents never accepted me and felt I was beneath them. They were pleasant enough in front of Lee, but when he left for OCS, I was left behind and saw the hidden side of them I had always known was there. I stayed in my room most of the time except for meals, with my excuse of studying. After the first week, I wanted to go back and stay with my parents until Lee returned. When I revealed that on the phone, Lee couldn't understand why I would want that and called his dad to ask if something was wrong. I was loading the dishwasher the next morning when his dad approached me, telling me I had no right to upset his son that way. I disliked him even more. His mother was always relatively quiet, and I learned it was because of her husband's anger and rage if she crossed him. I had started to feel sorry for her, knowing I would never live that way.

Lee's dad was still on a mission to get him released from the service and had his family doctor write a letter to the powers that be that he thought Lee was unstable and if he had to serve would possibly commit suicide. The letter was sent, and we waited for a decision.

I also learned that Lee was fearful of his dad, who would shout and curse if he didn't like something he said or did. Years later, I realized the reason we never went out to eat, even on our honeymoon, was that Lee was subjected to this anger many times at home meals and during the rage would become so scared he would go to the bathroom and throw up. This became a phobia that disallowed him to eat in front of people. It took years after he left home for this to minimize, but it did impact our social life. Lee was so tied to his parents that he wouldn't make any decisions without consulting them first, rather than me. The resentment in me was growing.

I did miss him and took my first flight ever to go across the country. The only flight I could get was first class. I still remember the outfit I wore: a navy knit dress, white gloves, and a navy felt hat with a leather white rose on the side. I looked stylish, I thought! When the attendant came to take drink orders (back then we called them stewardesses), I was twenty years old and had never had alcohol, and not knowing any names I looked at the guy next to me and said, "I'll have what he's having!"

It was a gin martini with olives. I almost spit it out, it was so bad! I took one sip and decided no more alcohol for me! After all, I was a Methodist! Funny, I sit here writing sipping my favorite Cabernet now!

When I arrived, we were so glad to see each other and were staying at a hotel in Oceanside. We enjoyed a night of passion and holding each other, thrilled to be together again. The next morning, I went downstairs to the diner and ordered breakfast, asking for scrambled eggs, crisp bacon, and grits. The waitress said," Honey, what is a grit?"

I had to resort to hashbrowns and thought how odd it was that people would eat potatoes for breakfast. During the early evening, I remember telling Lee my stomach hurt, and the next morning I told the waitress that I didn't want hashbrowns because they gave me a stomachache. I found out later I had gotten pregnant the first night we were together!

When the Navy finally decided to release Lee from service, he was stationed in San Diego and was told he would have discharge papers in three weeks, so I went to stay with him for two weeks that turned into three months. That's when I found out how slow the government is. I was constantly nauseated, and finally went to a doctor who congratulated us on being pregnant. We were thrilled, and I think my thoughts of staying married were solidified at that moment. Even though I wasn't really happy in the marriage and did not like his parents, I knew I would stay for this child, who was a boy, and my daughter, who arrived two and a half years later and make it work. That decision would last fourteen years.

Choosing the wrong man to marry causes pain and heartache for all involved. Such a major decision should never be taken lightly. Children suffer for the rest of their lives. They learn not to trust, they feel responsible, and they will more than likely deal with a stepparent who is a stranger invading their space with a birth parent and/or step siblings they have nothing in common with except a parent who chose another spouse. These are major situations we cause by picking the wrong husband or partner. It is life-altering for everyone, and many hurdles become part of everyone's lives. And unfortunately, many choose not to jump them.

CHAPTER 9

The Beginning and the Ending: Beware of Yankees!

It was a typical Macon day, filled with heat and humidity. I could always tell the humidity level by the frizz in my "natural" blonde hair! I was in my twenties, and my job in my "first life" was a part-time lab technician at Coliseum Hospital. My children were still small, and I felt they needed me home more than I needed a new car or more clothes. Looking back now, it was certainly not the right profession for me! You must be detailed and precise, and people who know me see me as all over the place, multi-tasking and being somewhat scatter-brained! The only part of that job I enjoyed was interaction with patients and their families—test tubes, microscopes, and machines that needed calibrating were not my thing!

Most of my co-workers were about the same age, and we took our job seriously but still managed to have fun and socialize. One day and without the lab administrator warning us, two men wearing suits approached me asking various questions, and I had been trying without success to get a machine that read blood sugar levels to work, and I was exasperated. One man, in a mild-mannered way, asked, "And what, young lady, may I ask are you doing?" My reply, in frustration, was, "Your guess is as good as mine!" He looked rather astonished, and they moved on.

I learned shortly thereafter that these guys were there to check out our accreditation status for the hospital. Lord, have mercy! I became the talk of the hospital that day, but we passed inspection in spite of it!

I had worked at the hospital for about three years after earning my degree. There was also a nursing school associated with the hospital and we shared friendships, some even continuing to this day. The hospital was located downtown with a large emergency room. This is where the word "stat" became a large part of our vocabulary. Ambulances were constantly coming and going, and we were called to draw blood from victims of gunshot wounds, stabbings, car wrecks, women having miscarriages, snakebites, and any kind of accident you can imagine. We rushed to do crossmatching for those needing blood immediately due to stab wounds or hemorrhaging for various reasons. We saw much trauma but had to be strong and not overreact during the mayhem.

The interns usually walked through the lab in the morning to get to the parking lot after pulling a long night shift. Once, one of them approached me and asked, "Have you ever had a Yankee dime?"

Being a Southern girl with Southern roots, I knew little about Yankees and really didn't care to know more. I immediately said, "No," and he leaned over and kissed me. My mind raced, and my thought was, "What the hell?"

As my eyes widened, he gave me a grin and walked out the door. I thought to myself, "another damn Yankee!" But he was cute!

One day, I had a requisition order to draw blood from a patient on the third floor. I wasn't prepared for what I would find there that would change my life forever. I loaded my tray with tubes of various sizes and colors and alcohol swabs and needles for the tests that were ordered. Just as I approached the closed door to the room, a sudden feeling of warmth and positive energy encompassed my entire body. I stood there a moment as I was taken aback, having never felt anything like it. The sensation filled my heart with love for whoever was behind that door.

I opened it slowly, walked over to the bed with my tray and observed an elderly lady with gray hair and years of wrinkles, with glasses that covered her tired eyes. She was large in stature and dressed in an oversized hospital gown. She didn't make eye contact as I proceeded to check her armband and said, "Ms. Davis, I'm here to draw blood from you."

She did not say anything but stared as I put the tourniquet on. As the needle pricked her skin, she started making loud guttural sounds without forming words, and immediately a nurse came in alerting me that she was deaf. I told her that someone should have told me. She also said Ms. Davis, whose first name was Minnie, had been brought to the ER from a nursing home in Jeffersonville, Georgia, with bleeding ulcers and had almost bled to death. The nurse held her arm while I drew blood and then left the room. Minnie and I were locked in a gaze, and I knew at that moment something special would transpire between us. The connection was immediate and would remain for the rest of her life. She proceeded to watch an old Western on television that I had interrupted, and I left the room still trying to understand the feelings I had for her. I later learned that her favorite shows were reruns of *Gunsmoke*—the same cowboy shows I watched as a child. I visited her every day at the hospital, and when I entered the room, we smiled at each other, and I knew the bond was strong and sensed she felt it, too.

One Sunday, while in church with Lee and our two young children, I sensed something was wrong and whispered to Lee that I had to go to the hospital, and I left in the middle of the sermon. When I entered Minnie's room the bed was empty, and my heart sank, thinking the worst. I went to the nurses' station fighting back tears and was told she had hemorrhaged again and was in surgery. My heart hurt as if she was a member of my family. I waited until she was out of surgery so she would know I was there and cared about her. When she was in a semi-awake state she smiled, and I held her hand as if to say, "It will be all right and I'm here for you."

When she was well enough to go back to the nursing home, I knew I would visit her as often as possible. She had become a big part of my life I couldn't quite grasp but couldn't let go.

My children were in kindergarten and first grade, and I planned my trips around their hours and my part-time work schedule. My first trip twenty miles down interstate 16 led me to a medium-sized brick facility with a large parking lot. Some residents were sitting outside, although I felt the sun was quite unbearable. I felt rather awkward and somewhat nervous, never having been to a nursing home before. I stopped at the desk and asked for Minnie's room with stares from others as if a stranger had come to town. The receptionist asked if I was a relative, but it didn't seem to matter as she led me down the long hall filled with older people who, like most of us, never thought they would wind up there. I knocked on the door, forgetting for a moment that she couldn't hear. I slowly opened it and when Minnie saw me, the love in her eyes and mine was immediate and smiles were exchanged. Even though we couldn't speak words, somehow, we knew what the other was thinking, and we both were overjoyed to be reunited.

At that instance, I saw another lady in the room, who I learned was Minnie's sister, Claudia. She also was a deaf-mute. Minnie managed to reassure Claudia with hand gestures that I was a nice person and not to be afraid. Minnie acted out with motions, as if playing charades, revealing that people would come into their room and go through their drawers and take things. I noticed there was not a television and knew how much she enjoyed the one in the hospital. So, on the following Sunday at Sunday school, I told the class my story and asked that we take up donations to buy one for their room. Everyone agreed to participate. I took the television and Minnie squealed with delight when she saw it, and I finally figured out how to set it up for them.

I also took a big calendar for their wall and would mark in red the days I would return to visit. I marked off the days that had passed and pointed to the red ones. I marked and gestured that those were the days I would return. Minnie and Claudia now had something to look forward to all week. I would go at least two days a week, making the thirty-minute drive back in the '70s when gas prices were through the roof! My husband, who would later become my ex, complained about the money it was costing, although he cared about them too.

Minnie and Claudia always ate in their room because they were distrustful of others, but I finally convinced Minnie to eat with me in the main dining room. I think she was thrilled to get out of the small room and have a dining companion. I met so many of the other residents who were delightful and eager to have someone notice them and share a smile or a few words that later became longer conversations as the years went by. Claudia was content to stay in the room and watch TV.

I finally started taking my small children, Lee and Julie, ages five and seven, to visit so I didn't have to rush back to Macon and pick them up from school. They were immediately welcomed with joy by all the older people, who adored them. Ms. Ann had only half a nose, as it was eaten by cancer, and she was constantly wiping it but loved our visits and hugging my children. "Baby" was a pleasant, overweight, and older guy who had mental issues and talked like a baby but loved to chat with us. Miss Nettie was an adorable Black lady with braids who wheeled herself down the halls and was always eager to greet us.

Once a strange incident occurred that is still a mystery. My son, Lee, had developed warts on his hand, which made him very self-conscious. One of the ladies in the home mentioned a man who could remove them because he was the "seventh son of the seventh son" and could rub them off! I was skeptical but thought it was worth a try . . . anything to make my son feel better. We went into the stranger's room, which was filled with bedside ointments and a strong scent of menthol. He was an old man with white hair and a long beard to match, and a face with well-earned wrinkles. We spoke pleasantries and he immediately took my son's little hand. He began to rub the warts and was chanting words I didn't understand. I smiled at him and thanked him as we left and had convinced myself it would never work. Two days later the warts were gone!

As Christmas was nearing, I took a small real tree and set it up in Minnie and Claudia's room so they could feel the spirit of Christmas. When I walked in with the tree, Minnie's eyes lit up as she grinned in a childlike manner. I bought toiletries, socks, sweaters, nightgowns, robes, and fun things that the kids and I would wrap in pretty Christmas paper and colorful bows and leave under the tree. Minnie and Claudia were like little kids and thrilled with excitement when I would bring in more wrapped gifts. The Sunday School class was eager to contribute once more. My kids got into the spirit and helped pick out gifts and couldn't wait to see the women's expressions when unwrapping the boxes! Minnie and Claudia had no living family and I often wondered if they had ever had a Christmas tree and experienced the joy Christmas brings before. My instincts made me think they didn't.

There was no one to ask about their younger years, which was sad. I firmly believe that all the love we were surrounded by during this experience led to my kids' love for older people and their desire to want to give back, as that time allowed them to see and learn the joy that giving brings. On one visit, as I walked down the hallway, the administrator, whom I had seen many times as I passed by his office, stopped me, and asked, "Why do you do this? We can't even get relatives of most of our other residents to visit and you are so loyal to people you didn't even know!"

My reply was genuine, explaining that I was led to do it and they needed someone to bring joy and love to their last few years on Earth.

Our journey together in life continued for over three years before I received a call from the nursing home administrator telling me Minnie had died suddenly. Our hearts were broken, and Julie and Lee cried; we grieved as if a family member had passed away. I attended the funeral in a tiny country church in Jeffersonville, Georgia, and as expected there were only a few people. The preacher was Pentecostal and was one of those who made it a stage for his antics, not even knowing Minnie! He occasionally banged his fist on the podium with, "Praise Jesus, praise the Almighty!"

My emotions were fragile, and I didn't need a sermon by a crazy man . . . after all, I am a Methodist! When the torture ended, I went to the bathroom, as we women do, and as I entered the stall, I asked in a demanding way, "Who was that preacher?" ready to blast off.

The lady washing her hands said, "Oh, he's my brother," to which I quickly replied, "Oh, he was great!"

Sorry, God, my halo got crooked for a moment! I still have a white ceramic cat Minnie made during a class at the nursing home that sits visibly in my overfilled closet; she was so thrilled to be able to give me a gift. But she could never know the profound gift of love she gave me with our spiritual connection that proceeded to change my life.

This was my first experience being led by the Holy Spirit and let me know that angels really do exist, and God uses us to help others in ways we couldn't imagine. I don't know why I was chosen to bring joy to Minnie's life, but she brought the same to mine. As they say, God works in mysterious ways, and I'm so glad he put us together. Without a word ever spoken we shared a special kind of love that only the heart understands.

Side note: My daughter, Julie, went on to become an occupational therapist at all three Mayo Clinics and worked with elderly patients. They adored her, one being Reverend Billy Graham, who always asked for her and presented her with an autographed copy of his book.

CHAPTER 10

Going Home to a Better Place...
No Shoes Needed

I was thirty years old when my life was changed forever. I got a call from my mother saying my dad had been sick for days and couldn't keep any food down. My first thought was a stomach virus, but I immediately made a doctor's appointment. When I picked him up at my childhood home and walked outside to the car, his skin and eyes were golden—the color of the sun's rays that day. My heart sank, and deep down I knew it was bad. Working as a lab tech at the hospital where I had graduated from lab tech school eight years prior offered me some knowledge of medical conditions.

When the lab results showed extreme elevations in bilirubin and liver enzymes, I knew it would be cancer. In fact, pancreatic cancer back in the '70s was a death sentence. This was my dad, the one who kidded with me and who tried to make my life happy the best way he knew how. I still wouldn't give in to cancer, and the doctor said he could try the Whipple procedure and remove small portions of his vital organs to try and stop the spread. I prayed so hard, but the day of the surgery I could see the bad news on the doctor's face as he entered the waiting room, where my mother and I sat, before he ever uttered a word. The cancer had spread, and all they did was sew him back up. My mother cried silently, and I felt a piece of my heart break off while trying to absorb what this meant. Daddy lived in pain for six months, grunting every day and unable to keep anything down. There was a drain inserted in his abdomen so we could collect the yellow bile that his liver could no longer process.

I visited him every day and read from the Bible because I had to know he was saved. He would say, "I'm so glad I believe that" and I was relieved.

He would crave things he had never tried before, and by the time I went to the store or restaurant to get it, he had changed his mind. The pain pills didn't help all that much, and finally we knew that he needed to go to the hospital for the relief only a morphine pump offered. Lee, my husband at the time, carried my dad in his arms from the parking lot. At that point, my dad weighed a mere sixty-seven pounds and couldn't even sit in a wheelchair. My heart was breaking, but I stayed strong for him and Mama.

The morning he died, I arrived with my fake happy face, and he was sitting up in bed. He asked for his shoes, and I asked him where he was going. He replied, "I'm going home," and later I realized he knew he was leaving the world that day.

He laid back down and his breathing became shallow, and I pushed the nurse's button in despair and fright. When she arrived, I knew by the look in her eyes it wouldn't be long now, and she suggested I call my Mama, who had just left to go home and feed the dogs. She didn't make it back in time. I was alone with him, holding his hand and telling him I loved him. My tears flowed as he took his last breath. He was only sixty-six years old. After Mama arrived with instructions of where his frail and lifeless body would go, I left for home. I still remember the numbness I felt walking into the hospital lobby and out the front door, wondering why people were talking and laughing while my world had just fallen apart.

Dealing with grief at any age is traumatic. Your mind goes to autopilot to protect it until acceptance can take place. How long that takes differs on an individual basis. I feel that the stage you are in currently helps or hinders your ability to move forward. I was thirty years old, and this was my first experience with the death of a parent, and it showed me the realization of mortality that we tend to deny. It changed me and made me realize that living in an unhappy marriage was not the future I wanted for my children or myself.

CHAPTER 11

Disney World and Decision Time

My daddy's death was a crucial chapter in the book of my life and prompted a decision I knew I had to make. When I was finally able to regain my composure after the funeral, I sat with Lee and told him we needed to talk. I tried to explain that I knew our marriage was not a good one. I told him that I realized now that mortality is real, and I wanted him to be happy with someone who adored him, and that was not me.

Our kids were depressed most of the time, and even though you think staying in a marriage for the kids is best, it is absolutely the worst-case scenario. They sense the unhappiness and stay on edge thinking a divorce may happen any time, and with that comes fear of the unknown. I think it creates distrust because they know by your actions you aren't being truthful. They would spend the night with friends and call in the middle of the night to come home. I knew I couldn't keep doing this to them.

I told Lee that if he would agree to therapy, I was willing to try. He always said that therapy was for "crazy people", and he wasn't crazy! He reluctantly agreed to go, so we found a young psychologist in Macon, and I made an appointment. It was apparent from our first session that Lee had little to say.

I was nervous and didn't know a thing about therapy or how to act or respond to his questions. Lee went a few times and said he wasn't going back and that it was a waste of money. I felt that this was the only way to figure out how to live the rest of my life, and I kept going for almost two years—even when our therapist, Jim, moved to Atlanta. That was when I learned who I was and tapped into my inner self for the first time. I had been like a budding rose all those years, not knowing how to open and bloom.

Jim slowly nurtured me, showing me my worth, and I found a strength that had been dormant for so long. The final blow to my marriage was when we had planned a vacation to Disney World to stay inside the park to give the kids something to look forward to for months. Lee was an insurance adjustor, and I was working part-time at the hospital, so we had to save for months to make it possible.

The day we were to leave, Lee came down the stairs with a suitcase and said, "I can't go, I can't do this."

I knew one of his phobias had kicked in, but told him, "You ARE going! You can't do this to our kids!"

He reluctantly drove us to Orlando, and after check-in refused to leave the room. For seven days he ate alone in the room and refused to go to the park. I knew what I had to do. When we returned home, I called Jim to tell him I couldn't take it anymore and was going to get a divorce. He replied, "I knew you would eventually come to this conclusion but knew it was your decision to make."

He also advised me that Lee was the personality that without me and the kids might decide to kill himself, and he wanted me to know the possibility was there. I told him that was beyond my control, to which he replied, "You're ready."

I told Lee I could no longer live this way and it wasn't fair to any of us. He became angry, and when we did sit with the kids to tell them, he responded that it was all my doing, and he didn't want a divorce. The kids were ages nine and eleven, and the year was 1981. My son reacted by saying he would kill himself and my daughter ran to her dad's arms crying. I was the villain, they thought, being too young to understand.

When Lee realized I was going through with the divorce, he said to me, "You'll never make it without me!"

I replied, "Watch me!"

As Jim had predicted, one day Lee called and asked me to meet him in the church chapel where we had married. I reluctantly agreed, and when I arrived, he proceeded to say that if I didn't come back, he was going to kill himself. I was mentally prepared and told him I would certainly hate that for our kids, but if that's what he felt he had to do, I couldn't stop him. That was the end of my marriage. And no, he didn't kill himself.

I could have stayed and been stuck for the rest of my life, but the hurdle I was facing was worth it to me. I had no money and had to work two jobs to pay my bills. The kids were still adjusting and blaming me for disrupting their lives. The divorce decree allowed me to stay in the house we were in unless I remarried. I had to pay all the utilities and expenses. One day, I came home, and the phone had been cut off for non-payment. I stood there and cried, trying to console and convince the kids it would be okay. I could have easily gone back to my ex, but I knew there had to be something better on the other side of this hurdle. And later I would find it.

I pictured a life of love with someone I would cherish and want to spend every moment with. I wanted to look forward to his car driving up after work and an embrace and have a conversation about our day. I wanted my children to see what real love and a good marriage should be . . . not what it shouldn't be.

Once you picture a new life in your mind and set that goal you will change what you do, how you act, how you react, and thoughts that enter your mind. When you let go of fear, opportunities await. Leave the past and enter the future where life will be different. No one is meant to live in misery with a safety net with holes in it. I was on my way to a new life and saw it as an adventure. It led to great things. The most important thing I learned is that until you learn to love yourself you aren't capable of loving others in the way that leads to a good relationship.

CHAPTER 12

Five Dollar Dance that Ended in Romance

When I was divorced in the '80s, churches really didn't know what to do with us. I remember telling my minister that I was getting a divorce, and even though we were "pillars of the church," he assured me no one would be shocked. I thought I was hiding my misery, but that was not the case. He suggested that we start a new Sunday school class for singles and appointed me president. It would consist of me, the blonde, Terri, the brunette, and Louise, the redhead with a temperament to match. The male members consisted of an older guy with that one piece of hair he was determined to keep by combing it to the side and across the top, a mama's boy who never grew up, and a sweet young guy who had been struck by lightning a few years before. A few others later joined us, but it was a mismatched group to say the least.

We frequently went to lunch after Sunday's sermon for companionship, and someone suggested we have a church dance as our Christmas party—after all, Methodists are allowed to dance. We would sell tickets for five dollars each. Louise asked me, "And who the hell are we going to dance with?"

I told her that if she knew some eligible men, she could certainly ask them. After pondering a few minutes, she said she knew a nice guy who was divorced and drove a nice car, even indicating we might just hit it off. I suggested she call him and if he would buy a ticket I would go to his office and get his five dollars. Ironically, his name was also Pat!

She called to tell me that Pat said to come by, so I ventured out to meet this divorced oral surgeon. He came out to the waiting room in his white coat, salt and pepper hair, and mustache, with sort of Dr. Zhivago looks. I could see the office girls peeking around from the desk area to size me up. I looked at him and thought he was handsome, and he looked at me thinking I was pretty. But the fact was, he was dating a girl from Atlanta, and I was dating a guy in North Carolina I had met at church but knew that relationship was coming to an end because I felt he would always put his two little girls first and I refused for my children to take a back seat. I told Pat when and where the dance would be and he pulled out five dollars and was interested enough to suggest we have dinner one night, to which I replied that would be nice.

The night of the dance came, and it was a "dud", and he didn't even show up. It wasn't really a date, so I didn't take it personally. About a week later, he called rather late at night to apologize for not coming with the excuse he had been out drinking that Saturday afternoon and didn't think it was right to come to the church with alcohol on his breath. I told him it was fine, that he missed a great time and I had kept his five dollars! Once again, he ended the conversation with: "Maybe we can have dinner one night," to which I once again agreed that would be nice. I started to feel he really was interested.

Meanwhile, as part of my decorating job at the flooring place I attended the Rug and Carpet Show in Atlanta at the

Merchandise Mart, which is an enormous event. Buyers come from all over the country, and by 6 p.m. your feet feel as if you've stomped grapes all day. And I needed wine, desperately. While in a showroom, I met a salesman who was cute and flirty, and asked me to have dinner with him. He was funny, made me laugh, and I had no plans except to find a bar with libations to help my throbbing and swollen feet. We went by taxi to a nice restaurant (after all, it was his expense account) and got acquainted and laughed a lot. On the drive back to my hotel he asked if he could come up to my room and received an emphatic "NO!"

He said he would come to Macon, and we would go out again. He called in a few days to say he and his boss were coming to the Air Force base nearby and wanted to have dinner with me, and I agreed. He called back the day before and asked if I had a girlfriend to bring along for his boss. I don't know what prompted me to ask if his boss was married, which he was, and I told him in no uncertain terms my friends didn't go out with married men.

On the afternoon of our date, I dressed nicely and took my kids to the cafeteria to eat and only had iced tea, knowing I was going out for a great meal. About thirty minutes before our date, he called and informed me he and his boss had gotten tied up and asked if we could go out the following night. My response was, "You know the number you just called? Don't you ever call it again!" I think the Scorpion in me kicked in being born in November. I explain it by saying: I'm "good as gold unless you cross me!" And cross me he did!

I hung up without saying goodbye and called my friend, Louise, the redhead, and told her what had happened. She was mad too, ironically being a Scorpion also, and suggested we go out and meet up with some of her other friends for drinks and dinner. At first, I told her no, feeling sorry for myself, but called right back and agreed. After all, I was already dressed and really hungry. How could I have known that night would change my life?

I had been divorced for about two years and never was a "bar hopper." It just didn't appeal to me, thinking men in bars were out for one thing and I wasn't interested in playing that movie scene. There was a small neighborhood *Cheers*-type bar nearby, and that's where Louise wanted to go. She mentioned that the "group," as she called it, gathered every Wednesday. They were a group of professional men, some married, some not, who met after work to inhale scotch and talk and laugh and, of course, watch women. When we entered the bar, I felt like I was on parade, and as I looked around, I saw Pat sitting on the upper tier at a table filled with women. I heard him say, "I know her," as if I was some prize. Louise and I kept walking and sat at a table with a couple she was friends with.

A little while later, Pat came to our table and hugged Louise, his friend, and smiled and shook my hand. After some conversation, we all decided to go to T.K. Tripp's to eat dinner and proceeded to get a large table for ten. Pat made sure he could sit next to me. That was the beginning of our courtship, as he asked me out the following weekend. His friends were fun, especially after some libations, and they accepted me into their "group." I was delighted, but still played it somewhat cool, not knowing where we were headed with this potential romance.

We went to fancy restaurants I never could have afforded, and the Elks Club, which was downtown and a favorite hangout. It was in a large historic area and was lovely in every sense of the word. The waitstaff was Black and wore tuxedos and I got to know them and loved them all. Looking back, I'm sure they knew many untold secrets about these guys!

This was in the mid '80s and we became the "darling couple" with bets on whether we would survive or not. Pat was thirteen years older than me and had three children of his own, with the two girls living with their mother in Atlanta and Pat's son living with him. He was waiting to enter college at the University of Georgia . . . Go Dawgs! Pat's reputation was one of a womanizer who drank too much. It wasn't my plan to change that, but I did.

We dated every night, staying out until one or two in the morning. It was as if we connected in a way he had never known, and we talked incessantly about everything. We used to observe couples sitting in restaurants looking bored who never talked to each other. We made a vow never to be like that and we weren't—even toward the end of our thirty-three years together.

I remember one night we were at the Elks Club and had just enough to drink to be crazy enough to jump in the pool with our clothes on and made out like crazy before he brought me home, both of us soaking wet. The kids were hysterical, saying there was a critter in the chimney. Somehow Pat managed to get a broom and discovered it was a flying squirrel, and all was calm in the world once more.

I took a chance with a divorcee with three children who weren't close to their dad, a womanizer of sorts, a man who drank too much, and who would have a struggle living in a home with my two children if the relationship worked out. I would enter his world of unknowns, but God sent him to me, and all our lives changed for the better.

CHAPTER 13

Anticipation, Apprehension, and Thirty Seconds of Bliss

I think Pat and I both felt after a few months that our connection was there to stay. Pat asked me to go to Hilton Head, South Carolina, for a weekend when my kids would be with their dad. We were sitting in the car in front of my house, and I proceeded to tell him that I did not intend to sleep with a man who was not seriously interested in me. He leaned over and kissed me to reassure me that he was. I agreed to go and was excited and scared. I went to our famous department store, Joseph N Neels, on Cherry Street in Macon, which still had the old elevator with the iron door that closed it, and a delightful Black lady with a pleasant smile who asked for your floor. I knew I couldn't really afford a nightie, but this was a special occasion! I tried on several and picked a short, lacy one in burgundy that fit my 115 pounds nicely. I have saved it all these years.

Friday afternoon arrived, and after Pat was finished seeing patients, we stopped by the Elks Club for a drink before our adventure began. He had a dirty martini, and I had a margarita to calm my nerves! I think we both were apprehensive but started the journey of three hours down I-16. I bought the Carpenters' latest CD with a song that is a favorite to this day: "Make Believe It's Your First Time and I'll Make Believe It's Mine." When we arrived at the Mariner's Inn on the island it was late, but we needed to eat and were able to get something simple before heading to our room. I think I was so nervous that the food didn't go down, but with the help of another margarita I managed to walk to the door.

When Pat opened it and I saw the king-sized bed, I froze for a minute and was tempted to run but didn't. Thoughts were racing through my mind: "Did I really want to do this . . . was I ready to give myself to someone again . . . would he think less of me . . . would he tell his friends . . . was I just a trophy?"

I'd never been so nervous. We took turns in the bathroom, and I changed into my nightie and walked out. I could see the passion in his eyes, and when I laid down next to him the intimacy only lasted about thirty seconds. He was embarrassed and I was confused but longed for sleep after being so stressed out all day.

The next day was strange, and I sensed a coolness on his part and thought to myself that I was just another notch on his belt he could tell the guys about. We laid in the sun and started drinking in the early afternoon and into the night, as I really needed something to numb my thoughts.

At dinner, Pat started talking about his kids and his regrets of not being close to his youngest daughter and his eyes filled with tears. I learned that when he and his wife first married, he was a dentist and entered the Air Force as an officer. They were into their first year of marriage and he was lucky enough to be stationed at Aviano Air Force Base in Italy. He learned to snow ski and loved classical music. He and his buddies and their wives would take turns at each other's homes on Sunday afternoons playing their favorite records.

One Sunday, his wife opted out with a headache and Pat went alone. Remembering that he had forgotten a record, he returned home to find a superior officer in bed with his wife. She said she was in love with him, but back in the '60s and in a foreign country, divorces didn't happen. They stayed together for over twenty years, and he was recruited to Macon from the Mayo Clinic in Rochester, Minnesota, where he had just finished his residency in oral surgery. He felt payback was fair play and had a few affairs himself, and eventually they divorced.

I sensed the pain Pat was feeling and realized that he over-drank to ease it. We went back to our room and just held each other until the morning came. On the long drive back to Macon we were both rather quiet, and I felt it was probably the end of what could have been a relationship. We hugged goodbye and I left him with a sadness we both felt.

A week went by with no communication until I received a Valentine from him in the mail. It was generic with a sweet note just short of an apology. He called a few days later with the excuse of redecorating his office, and said he wanted me to be the one to do it. I went over in my business suit, determined to make it strictly business except for the prolonged hug when we saw each other. I took measurements of the rooms and told him I would get back to him. When I did, he asked me to dinner, which I agreed to, and we rekindled our relationship and never looked back. That was February of 1987, and I realized that God had a hand in this and wanted us to be together. A few of my friends told me later they would never have put us together, knowing how different we were. We married August 15, 1987.

*So, don't listen to your friends but to your head and heart instead. If there is a perfect marriage, we had it. We never wanted to be apart and proved to ourselves that real love does exist. Don't deny yourself the opportunity by staying in a bad relationship you know isn't working but move on to one that can. I also feel I entered Pat's life as part of God's plan to bring joy to his life. He was a good man, struggling. I feel I was an angel led to him and he gave me a love I had never known.

CHAPTER 14

*Falling Inn Love . . .
The Seed Was Planted*

One Sunday morning, I was reading the *Macon Telegraph*, and the front page featured a story on the Susina Inn in Thomasville, Georgia. The exterior looked just like Tara from *Gone with the Wind*, being white and grandiose with large columns. I continued to read with growing excitement and learned they also served evening meals for their guests who, after strolling through the beautiful grounds during the day, would want to enjoy a nice dinner. I knew I wanted to go and shared my enthusiasm, and Pat agreed. He was always ready for a new adventure and great food. We had become foodies at this point in our marriage of five years. We made reservations for the weekend and loaded the car for the three-hour drive.

As we approached the Southern mansion from the long driveway, my heart was beating fast with excitement. We were greeted with Southern hospitality and climbed the grand staircase, being led to our room. A four-poster bed and antiques adorned the light-filled room, and a bottle of port was on the nightstand. We wandered around the lovely, manicured grounds anticipating our dinner that awaited. The dining room consisted of a perfectly set large dining table with twelve matching mahogany chairs. The food was amazing, and we loved meeting new people from different towns and there was never a lag in conversation.

Little did I know that I returned to Macon with a seed planted inside of me; a desire to open our own inn would soon start to sprout. I loved the experience so much that whenever we traveled anywhere, I would refer to my new guidebook and pick inns rather than hotels. We stayed in some great ones, but one in Boston was really lacking. We were at an oral surgery convention, and I picked out a bed and breakfast, having very few options. When we arrived with too much luggage (typical for me), we had to carry it three flights to our bedroom. The room was small and had some of the owner's clothes in the closet. She only rented two rooms and we were the only guests. Breakfast was in the kitchen and consisted of yogurt and weird and healthy food, and being from the South, we were accustomed to bacon and eggs. We suffered through it, and the owner turned out to be a psychologist who was going through a divorce. I wound up counseling her since I had been through it myself. I did learn that there really is such a thing as Southern hospitality that is only done in the south, and it made me love my roots even more.

Another trip that changed our lives was an inn in Valle Crucis, North Carolina. My inn guidebook piqued my interest with an inn there, The Mast Farm Inn, where they grow their own vegetables for their dinners and have an abundance of goats. I really wanted us to stay there and was disappointed when I called to learn they were full. They did, however, recommend a new inn that had just opened, The Inn at the Taylor House. I called and booked it, and upon arrival pictured what an old white farmhouse with chickens and goats must have looked like in previous days. This was far from it. The innkeeper was Chip Wilson, who had moved from Buckhead, Atlanta, and was married to a renowned chef at one of Atlanta's five-star restaurants. The place was immaculate and filled with antiques, Oriental rugs, and gorgeous art, and the food was to die for. Chip was so congenial. We loved sitting in the porch rockers in the afternoons, sipping wine, and learning about innkeeping.

I felt the seed to open our own inn growing faster inside me. We revisited that inn many times and finally decided one day we would own a bed and breakfast. Chip suggested we join the Professional Innkeepers of America and attend their conferences to learn more. We did just that, and I even enrolled in a two-year culinary school at a nearby college. The curriculum was from the National Restaurant Association and involved studying followed by tests. The first day of class, I met the teacher, who I knew previously had run a school lunchroom cafeteria, and I knew that was not what I needed. I walked down to the vice president's office and asked to speak with him. I told him that I didn't need to learn to fry pork chops one more time and suggested I do my practical under a trained chef at the City Club in Macon or I would "get the hell out of dodge." I informed him that I was willing to give him two years of my life and was probably one of the few who were paying tuition. Many students there got a check just for being in school. He agreed and my culinary career began.

I was back in school at age forty-five. I would go to class in the morning and leave at lunch to head to the City Club, of which we were members. The chef was a young guy they had recruited from the Occidental Hotel in Washington, DC. He didn't quite know what to do with me, and I chopped a lot of onions and peeled a lot of fruit until we figured out my role. The irony was that around 5:00 p.m., I would leave the hot kitchen, change clothes, and meet our friends out front in the beautiful and elegant restaurant, where I was treated just like any other member. The good thing was, I knew what looked good that day and ordered for us. That was an unforgettable opportunity that led to a cooking school later.

To reach a goal you must prepare, and there are many steps required to reach the top of the mountain. There may be many stopping points but keep the focus and dream alive and keep climbing. When you do and look down at your accomplishments, you may even amaze yourself.

CHAPTER 15

Twilight Zone and Being Arrested

My ex remarried within a year of our divorce to a nice lady with kids, but that only lasted a short while. He then married again to an unstable woman I will refer to as Amy, to protect her son who was small at the time. It was obvious she didn't like me from the get-go. After five years she became involved with the underground railroad and Fay Yeager, as seen on TV. Women would accuse husbands and other men in the community of child molestation and other horrible acts and then proceed to hide the children, changing their names and identities. She even accused one of our Methodist churches of sacrificing a baby at the altar, accused our Sunday school teacher of molesting children, and accused Lee of killing babies and burying them in the backyard. I think I hear the *Twilight Zone* music playing.

The Georgia Bureau of Investigations (GBI) finally located them by helicopter and confiscated Amy's notebook that had names of all the people she was accusing. Lee did divorce her, with good reason. Needless to say, my kids went through an ordeal trying to adjust to stepmothers and step siblings.

During Lee's marriage to Amy, one weekend Julie had stayed with her dad and was to be home that afternoon. When it became late, I called the house to speak to Lee and Amy answered. I asked where Julie was, and she said she did not know. I told her she should know since she spent the weekend there. She said, "Listen bitch, I don't have to talk to you," and hung up the phone.

I was shocked, to say the least. I told Pat to wait at home in case Julie returned and I got in my car and drove to their house a few miles away.

The driveway was steep, and as I drove up and got out of the car, I could see Amy walk past the door and enter the laundry room. I rang the bell, and she jerked the door open and without a word started slapping my face and trying to push me backward down the driveway. I knew if I touched her, I would be as guilty as she, so I didn't overreact and focused on steadying my feet. Suddenly, it was as if Amy came to her senses, stopped, looked at me and turned around, and walked back inside without speaking a word. It was as if she came out of a trance! I was amazed and dumbfounded at this, but mad enough to go to a neighbor's house and call the police. It happened on a Sunday afternoon, so the officer suggested I come to the station the next day to file a report. I did, and he said he would issue a warrant and have her brought in.

Two days later, I was at my place of employment, having become an interior designer and working at a local flooring place, when a policeman walked in and asked if I was Mrs. Allen. When I said I was he said he had a warrant against me, and I needed to come with him to the station. I was shocked, knowing I never touched her, and he also said she had taken out a restraining order against me! Cue more *Twilight Zone* music playing. I followed his car to the police station dressed in my business suit, and the other policemen looked shocked to see a professional lady in a business suit walk in. I had to walk past the inmates who were whistling and making comments as I went down a hallway to be fingerprinted. I then had my mug shot taken and think I had a big grin, thinking how ridiculous it all was. A court date was set, and my Pat, Amy, and my ex appeared before the judge. She even had an attorney with her who happened to be one of my high school "friends!" Traitor . . . LOL! The case was thrown out, but the judge told us to stay away from each other. He didn't have to worry about that! I resented the fact that my ex had again put me in a difficult situation that I had to try and explain to my kids.

An incident occurred months later when I arrived at the parking lot at our local hospital for a doctor's appointment. I stepped out of my car and put the key in the door to lock it. Suddenly, a feeling of coldness and a fear I couldn't describe encompassed my body. I finally shook it off, and when I turned around and walked toward the building, Amy and her mother were glaring at me, and I knew it had been the force of evil I felt. It was totally the opposite of the feeling of warmth and love that occurred with Minnie, the deaf-mute lady, who was a patient in the same hospital.

God had shown me that BOTH good and evil really do exist, and I experienced the feelings that come with both. We want to always think there is good in everyone, but I have learned otherwise. Bad snakes have stripes and can be identified . . . bad people look like you and me.

CHAPTER 16

Gorgeous Sunsets and Evil Hexes

In my last month of culinary school, I wanted something more exciting to finish my internship and decided to call Chef Tell Erhardt at the Grand Old House on Grand Cayman Island. Pat and I had eaten there a few times when we were on a scuba diving trip, and it was fabulous. And the setting was beautiful, right on the beach with gorgeous sunsets and soft, lapping waves on the turquoise water. Chef didn't know me from Adam, or should I say Eve, but I felt compelled to call. I was prepared for the operator to put me off as if a crazy lady trying to speak to a TV celebrity chef who was a regular on the daytime show *Regis and Kathie Lee*. To my surprise, she asked me to hold on. He came to the phone, and I told him I was finishing culinary school and offered to give him free labor for a month if he would train me. My mind and heart were racing when he asked, "When do you want to come?" We settled on May, and the year was 1994. I was so excited and couldn't wait to share the news with Pat.

Once I hung up the phone, it dawned on me that I had nowhere to stay and started calling various hotels. Of course, they had no space for a thirty-day rental. This was the days before Airbnb and VRBO. Finally, after explaining my situation to one of the hotel managers, she said she knew a lady school-teacher who was getting a divorce and had mentioned she might be willing to rent a room for income. I got her number and called immediately. Her name was Marilyn, and I immediately loved her Scottish accent and humor. We settled on a price and the date of my arrival. Pat was very supportive, and although we had never been apart in our ten years of marriage, I knew deep down I had to do this.

The day I arrived on Grand Cayman Island, I was thrilled to be there. The humidity immediately hit me, and I knew I would have thirty days of bad hair. I arrived midday and had to wait until after school was out for Marilyn to pick me up. Finally, in walked this diminutive lady with stocky legs and red hair. We immediately connected and she took my luggage as if she were a porter. Her two daughters, Lorna and Kate, aged thirteen and fifteen, were waiting in the car. We started off in the little four door sedan that became my only source of travel and little did I know the adventure that was about to begin.

When we arrived at the house, which was very nice and in a nice neighborhood only a few blocks from the beach, I walked into the air-conditioned home with tile floors and lots of windows and natural light. Marilyn showed me to the largest bedroom that had been hers, and I noticed the entire closet was cleaned out for me. I told her I was happy to take the third bedroom, but she refused. That made the girls double up together and I felt bad, but it was done. I was tired and fell asleep early that night, with only little time to get acquainted with Marilyn and the girls.

The next morning the three of them headed off to school, and afterward Marilyn took me to meet Chef Tell. I was nervous but excited to actually be there in his kitchen. He was very cordial and downright flirty, but I had zero interest. He offered to take me home, but I told him my ride would be back soon. I got to walk around and meet the cooks and staff and was struck by how hot and steamy the kitchen was. The only commercial kitchen I had worked in was the City Club in Macon with great air conditioning. I'm very hot-natured but knew I could struggle through.

There was a window with a view of the ocean and the most incredible sunsets I've ever seen. It was as if I could reach out and touch this incredible, massive ball of orange and reds that dipped down and disappeared in the ocean. When Marilyn and I finally had time to get acquainted at the house, she suggested we have tea in the afternoon. I told her I really didn't care for hot tea, and she proceeded to educate me on the British tradition that meant refreshments, and that biscuits referred to cookies and pastries and not hot buttered Southern biscuits I grew up on. So, in the late afternoons, before I went to the restaurant, I would have Tia Maria as my drink of choice until I realized I wasn't sleeping due to the amount of caffeine I was consuming! The little snack always helped me get through the mad evening rush at the Grand Old House. I finally had to get off the Tia Maria.

Marilyn soon felt comfortable enough to share the incidents that led to her impending divorce that wasn't yet settled. She told me that her husband had gotten involved with a woman from Trinidad he had met at a Cayman festival. She was involved in a cult-type religion, and she and Marilyn's husband would dance around in the yard to put a hex on the house and Marilyn. After my mouth was able to close, I listened. She was followed by this woman at various times and her husband moved in with her.

Marilyn had never known much about divorce, especially in a foreign country, and didn't know what, if anything, she, and the girls were entitled to. This was where I came to bat. I knew our laws but not theirs, so I proceeded to find out from the locals. Surely, with minor children she could keep the house. It was all negotiable, according to the weak laws. She had an income as a teacher and wasn't going to be destitute.

Marilyn and I became close and laughed a lot. Her personality and mine seemed to fit perfectly. One Saturday morning when her husband came to pick up the girls, I opened the door, and when our eyes met it was as if good met evil in a stare-down. I think he felt my strength and I felt his weakness. The cult woman wasn't there, and some of the brainwashing left him for the few moments it took to gather the girls. He knew I was there to fight for Marilyn if it came to that.

When the girls returned on Sunday afternoon, Marilyn and I sat with them in the great room. It was my chance to talk about my divorce and how confused and sad my kids were at first, but how strong they became and what a much better life they now had since I found the man I was happy with and was meant to be with. They listened intently and I was speaking words of wisdom and I remember thinking, "Where is this coming from?" And at that moment, I realized that I wasn't there to learn to cook; I was there to help this family. God had sent me on a mission, and before my thirty days were up, I did accomplish it. Marilyn got the house and alimony.

Meanwhile, back in the hot kitchen. I learned a lot about cooking seafood and making sauces and even gravlax. I worked alongside the pastry chef and learned to make a mean chocolate mousse and golden pastries. My eyes were really opened to the lack of sanitation and health inspections in third world countries and on the islands. The bread was put in a proofer overnight and were treats for tiny roaches. The kitchen was so hot that sometimes sweat became part of the salad. When Pat came to visit and wanted to eat there, I told him, "No way!" I'm sure it has improved since then as it was sold a few times since then.

I look back now and think Marilyn and I must have looked like two cartoon characters in a Fred Flintstone car, and I must smile. Once again, the Holy Spirit sent me on a journey never to be forgotten. I lost touch with Marilyn once we opened the inn and would love to know how her life progressed. I know she went back to Edinburgh as a stronger woman.

Having the courage to ask for what you want is so important. I was prepared for Chef Tell to say, "no way," but I took a chance and was allowed to touch the lives of people who were in need. Always think positive and you'll be amazed at what you can accomplish. Be a risk taker!

CHAPTER 17

Crazy Culinary Student and the Microphone . . . the Bus Rolled On

In anticipation of opening an inn and during my culinary training, the National Restaurant Association selected a culinary student in each school to be chosen and awarded the Student of Excellence award. They would be asked to attend the National Restaurant Show held in Chicago, where they would be given a few minutes to speak before receiving their certificate. I was chosen and thrilled to attend a show where "anybody who was anybody" in this business would be seen. Pat was a proud husband when we arrived in the windy city, which lived up to its name.

The next morning, I had seminars to attend, one with Herman Cain, who was CEO of Godfather's Pizza at the time. He told his story of humble beginnings; his mother was a maid, and his father was a janitor of sorts. Growing up poor, he never had dreams but felt he would follow in their footsteps and the shoes wouldn't be hard to fill.

Herman went on to say that a white man and someone who knew his dad approached him to ask what he was going to do when he finished high school, to which he replied, "I'll get a job."

The nice man told him he would not because he was going to college. Herman, of course, was flabbergasted and asked how on Earth he could do that, and the man told him he was going to get a scholarship. He asked Herman what his hardest subject in school was, and learned it was math, to which the man said, "That's what you will major in."

As it turned out, that's exactly what happened. He became an employee of Pillsbury, who owned Burger King at that time. He managed 400 stores and increased profits substantially and was then offered the position of CEO of Godfather's Pizza. He increased profits there and made a name for himself in the pizza industry.

When Herman spoke with his gentle tone, he described his journey in life like a bus with wheels that just kept rolling. He made a few stops along the way but didn't depart until the final destination felt right. I identified with Herman in that I started out as a lab technician, became an interior designer, was a food critic for the *Macon Telegraph*, and then had plans to open a bed and breakfast. My time on the bus wasn't over yet.

When I got the microphone the night of the event with 3,000 people attending, including Paul Prudhomme, J.W (Bill) Marriott, and Lou Holtz, to name a few, I spoke of my journey in life, referencing Herman's bus, and was filled with passion as I spoke about life. When the guy came for the microphone, I quipped, "Just one more minute, I'm almost done," as the audience laughed and applauded loudly when I finally gave up the mic.

After the dinner, we meandered around and Bill Marriott came over to me and said, "Young lady, you were great and will do great things, and anytime you get the chance to get in front of a microphone, take it."

I was shocked and thrilled that someone so successful would single me out to offer a compliment. After all, how many Marriott properties are there worldwide? My inn adventure was about to begin.

Having a goal in life is so important; otherwise, you live mundanely with what the universe offers everyone. But remaining focused on a goal will mentally prepare you to take the steps to lead you to your destination. Just like Herman Cain, figure out where you want the bus to stop, and make sure that you are the one behind the steering wheel. I've never agreed with the "if it's meant to be" philosophy. Someone must be in the driver's seat, and that needs to be you to make things happen!

CHAPTER 18

The Find, the Neighbor, and the Hate Mail

I was forty-six years old and happily married. In our quest to find a bed and breakfast whenever Pat and I traveled that was near a small town, I would leave a card with a local realtor asking that if anything desirable or affordable came on the market to please let me know. This was in the early 1990s, and the only phones were home and office. Can you believe we ever existed without them?

I received a call one Thursday in July from a realtor named David, who said that a house in Highlands, North Carolina, was coming on the market and he thought it would be perfect for us. It was an older white farmhouse with beautiful grounds in the downtown area. I couldn't wait to come see it! The only drawback was it was Fourth of July and the busiest weekend of the year in Highlands. There were no rooms to be found, but I didn't want the house to get sold without us seeing it first. I made calls to lodging places in the nearby areas, and the only room available was in the Lake Rabun area about an hour away from Highlands.

There were no computers yet, so no photos or reviews were available. I reserved the room, and when we drove up, I was reluctant to go in as it lacked maintenance in the worst way. When we entered the lobby, we noticed that men were gathered in front of the TV drinking beer, and at least one had his shirt off. They were shouting, and maybe there was a car race or something on, but we didn't hang around long enough to see.

We got our room key, and upon opening the door saw a full-size bed with a floral polyester spread with cigarette burns. The closet had a hole in it, making me think of Norman Bates's eyeball looking through. When we pulled back the sheets there was hair in the bed. I was appalled and called the manager. He came up and said, "Those damn Mexicans, I told them to clean this room!"

He and I changed the sheets, but Pat and I slept in our clothes and left at the first light of day. I couldn't wait to have breakfast and head up the mountain to Highlands.

We met with our realtor David, and he had a few other things lined up for us to see. The town and traffic were unreal in a small town that only needed one red light. Our first stop was the farmhouse and I loved it, but my Pat said he grew up in an old house and he knew the maintenance involved and wanted to keep looking. It's ironic that twenty-eight years later, I see that house every morning . . . more to come on that later. We saw the other areas of town and none of the houses really were what I had hoped we would find.

After a brief lunch, David said he wanted to show us one more house that was coming on the market soon. It was a little more than our budget, but I wanted to see it and Pat agreed. We drove a couple of miles out of town, and when we approached the white house sitting on a high hill, I knew without a doubt that was it! My heart skipped beats and my adrenaline was raging. The minute David opened the large front door to expose the mountain view, I said, "This is it; we are buying this house!" I had not even seen the rest, but my heart was filled with love and adoration for the house. I would later learn the reason.

The floor plan turned out to be perfect. There were three-bedroom suites on the main floor and room for expansion upstairs, which would later become our honeymoon suite. There was a large sunroom across the entire back of the house, which could be our dining porch with a view. A nice surprise was a back staircase from the kitchen that led to a huge storage room that would house our commercial refrigerator and pantry items, and across the hall was another great room with a fireplace and a small bedroom and shower and a covered porch that would be our living quarters separate from the guests. There was a three-car garage, workshop, and huge laundry area. The house sat on two acres, and I knew we could have a perennial garden and a waterfall and koi pond beneath huge boulders. My mind was on steroids!

My heart was racing as I ran through, knowing this was perfect. The issue would be the extra money outside our budget, and we both knew Pat would have to continue his practice for a while to pay the bills. We signed the offer to purchase and made it contingent on the septic being approved for more bedrooms. Looking back now, I'm glad we didn't get all the bedrooms. We had enough to take care of! Changes would come later.

One of the neighbors, George, got word we were going to open a bed and breakfast and started calling me in Macon every Sunday night to complain. He told me that we were going to ruin the neighborhood with traffic, delivery trucks, and noisy people. I explained that there would be no delivery trucks, knowing Pat would stop by Sam's Wholesale Club on Friday afternoons and bring supplies, and that as far as cars, the current owners had two businesses in town, two teenagers, and a young son and they were back and forth all day. I also told him our rates would be high enough to attract professionals and not the "young and restless." He wouldn't accept anything I said, and even stirred up the neighbors, the majority being elderly, who had owned homes there for many years and were second homeowners. Hate mail started coming, and my sweet Pat asked me why we wanted to go into a neighborhood where people already hated us and didn't even know us yet. All I said was, "We're going," and I knew beyond a shadow of a doubt that we were, and it was meant to be.

The last call I had from George was more harassment, and once I asked if I could call him George and he agreed, I asked, "George, are you a man of faith?" After a few seconds, he said he was, and I proceeded to tell him that everything inside of me said to do this and we were coming. He gave the old threat of getting an attorney, and I proceeded to tell him to give me the date and time and we would see him in court.

We were still in due diligence waiting on septic evaluation when I got a call from our closing attorney, Jack, in Highlands. He was almost ecstatic and couldn't wait to tell me, "Pat, I almost fell off my chair this morning! I went way back and researched the original deed, and it states: 'This is a residential neighborhood, and the only commercial use can be a HOTEL.' We got 'em!" That solidified my belief in doing this, and Pat was starting to come around.

Another amazing fact was that we were told that prior to the current owners, the home was willed to a Christian Ministry Club, and when they were facing financial troubles sent two thugs to burn the house down for the insurance money, and they burned the one across the street by mistake. They were later caught in Greenville, South Carolina, for doing the same thing. When the elderly little lady next door told me that story, I had goosebumps and more affirmation that the house was there for a reason, and I would quickly learn that reason.

Determination and not allowing bullies to control you or frighten you can lead to amazing results. If you truly believe in something, go for it, and jump the hurdle! Otherwise, you miss great opportunities in life.

CHAPTER 19

Preparation, Opening Jitters, Grits, and Granola

Meanwhile, back in Macon, my Pat was rather skeptical about how all of this would play out, and my main concern was being apart until he could retire. Our love was so strong, and the thought of being without him on Monday, Tuesday, Wednesday, and Thursday each week made my heart hurt. We always had breakfast, lunch, and dinner together every day for our ten years of marriage and I didn't know how I could be without him . . . I just knew I had to do this.

We had played around with names for the inn, and I knew I didn't want "mountain" or something similar but one with a different and unique connotation. One Sunday, while singing hymns in our Methodist Church, one referred to the Morning Star (Jesus) and I knew that was it: *The Morning Star Inn.* I later learned that many guests came because of the name.

We finally got septic approval (although less than I hoped for) and eventually the neighbors backed off, although George went to his grave hating me. There was so much to be done, getting ready to open.

That was August 1994 and I wanted to open by October for leaf season. Little did I know how much work was involved, but we took it one day at a time. I had furniture, linens, and accessories to buy, keeping in mind the needs of our guests. We would place two truffles on the bedside table and do turndown before the guests returned from dinner. I decided to name each room after stars and found plastic glow in the dark adhesive stars and mounted one on each ceiling. I came up with a little poem on a card for the bedside table in each room that read: "We are delighted you're here and bid you goodnight, the Morning Star appears above you when you turn out the light."

I found a handyman to put locks on each pocket door of each guestroom which wasn't easy to do. Pat was busy at work, since the summer was a time with kids out of school and teenagers needing their wisdom teeth removed. My friend, Cyndi, came from Macon to help some, but I was pretty much on my own. It's amazing how much energy you can muster when determination takes over your body and brain! I remember one day being so tired that I laid down in the new hammock I had put up between two large oak trees and fell asleep. It was fifty-nine degrees outside, and I woke up with a sunburned face. It was my first revelation that at 4,100 feet of elevation, we are closer to the sun!

Another item to be addressed was creating a breakfast menu. I learned a lot in culinary school, but not how to make a gourmet breakfast. I started researching inn recipe cookbooks and remembered an egg dish that had been our favorite at an inn in Valle Crucis, North Carolina. That would be my first entrée, followed by an apple French toast served with warm maple syrup. I knew I needed a granola as a starter, and not being able to find one I liked, came up with my own that not only was delicious but filled the inn with wonderful smells of cinnamon. I was naïve enough to think I only needed two perfect breakfasts because I assumed that guests would leave after two days . . . was I ever wrong! More on that later.

That was in September, and October was fast approaching. I was so intent on finishing the rooms that marketing never entered my mind. The only thing I did was go by the Chamber of Commerce to inform them of our existence, and I contacted the other inns in the area because I was anxious to meet other innkeepers. I knew I had to create a logo and brochure. That took time and effort, and I wrote the description myself. It was months before I realized I didn't know Shortoff Mountain from Whiteside Mountain, and that our view was of Shortoff, not Whiteside, as I had written in the brochure in error. Luckily, no one complained. After all, I didn't really know Highlands, having only been there twice before.

I also hadn't thought about a housekeeper, and trying to find one in October was a "duh" revelation. Initially, my sister came to help. On October 16, 1994, we had the pantry packed, the refrigerator was full, the rooms were ready, fresh flowers adorned the coffee table and dining table, and guests were coming thanks to sheer overflow from other inns who were booked. We planned to have wine and hors d'oeuvres every afternoon so the guests could linger, and we could get acquainted.

When the first car drove up, Pat and I were excited but anxious. Would they like us, our place, our food, our hospitality? All the guests were so gracious and complimentary when we showed them to their rooms. Soft piano music from Emile Pandolfi became a favorite as we set the tone for guests to relax.

I'm not sure I slept at all, knowing my first breakfast was finally going to happen. Pat had come up with a cheese grits recipe to accompany my signature Southwestern egg casserole.

We also baked little biscuits in miniature pans that had more butter than flour and were always a favorite. I found a wonderful muffin recipe filled with carrots and walnuts, and aptly named them Morning Star Muffins, which quickly became a guest favorite. We had put the coffee pot in the sunroom with air pots (containers that keep coffee hot) so guests could enjoy the scenery while waiting for their plates to be served. All the while we were behind closed doors in a tiny galley kitchen rapidly preparing our morning delights. We began service with a small ramekin of my original granola topped with diced granny smith apples and a small dollop of vanilla yogurt. Meanwhile, I went back to the kitchen to plate the egg dish, bacon rubbed with brown sugar or maple syrup, Pat's cheese grits, two tiny biscuits or a muffin, and a strawberry fan for garnish. I must admit, it was a pretty presentation and everything on the plate was delicious.

The guests that first weekend were delightful, one even shared a bottle of champagne to toast our success. I still have the cork framed along with all their names and the date. They loved the entire experience and would return many times over the years. On Sunday, after everyone had checked out, we were exhausted but knew we would be successful and had something special. This was back in the olden days before computers and cell phones, so communication was by real phones only. We never had to advertise because word-of-mouth and overflow kept us full. When the guests departed on Sundays, Pat and I would venture out for lunch at Wolfgang's Restaurant which at the time offered a New Orleans-style brunch. We would then return for a well-deserved nap.

As weeks went by, guests wanted to stay longer than two days, so I had to dust off the innkeepers' cookbooks for more breakfast entrees. Some favorites became spinach pie that I served with broiled tomatoes topped with Romano cheese or smoked salmon in puffed pastry and warm cream cheese and capers. I had the idea that one day I would do a cookbook, and asked my guests to send family favorites so they could be included. I was adamant that I didn't want casseroles with cream of chicken soup, just original favorites. I would later publish my first cookbook, *Whisk Upon a Star*, which sold out quickly. Another cookbook, *Mouth of the South*, would follow years later.

We had seven years of enjoyment with our guests who returned time and time again, and I wouldn't trade those years for anything. Hard work isn't so hard when you have a true passion for what you do. Pat loved it and was the perfect host, and everyone loved him, including me.

A funny story about my granola: At a seminar for innkeepers there was a contest sponsored by the National Baking Association to find the best granola from any inn in the entire country, and we were to bring a sample of our granola to be judged. The only problem was when Pat and I arrived in Baltimore, I had forgotten my bag of granola. I was so disappointed, but adrenaline kicked in and I took a taxi to the grocery store, bought ingredients, and somehow found a toaster oven to use. The smell of cinnamon permeated the breakfast area with my recipe. When they announced I had won, I was amazed and delighted! After all, I was competing with innkeepers nationwide with many more years in business than me. Part of the prize was being placed in the Walnut Acres mail order catalog, and I got lots of orders and many nice handwritten notes expressing their love for my granola. The recipe is at the end of my book.

Sometimes you must step out and take a leap of faith and belief in yourself. I really didn't know if our guests would love our place, the food, or us; I just knew I would make it the way I imagined I would like it. It was a dream I had in my mind, and I kept seeing it become a reality. Hard work and determination got me to the final destination. Dream it, envision it, set a goal, and make it happen.

CHAPTER 20

Happy Tunes Filled with Tears

As I mentioned in an earlier chapter, the house that became the *Morning Star Inn* was to be burned for insurance money by a Christian ministry group, but the wrong one was burned by mistake. The elderly lady across the street told me she looked out the window one morning to see flames at the house next door. At that time, the fire department in Highlands was voluntary, so the "wrong" house burned to the ground. There were so many things that fell into place to allow our inn to come to be. Many guests would often tell me they were led to the *Morning Star Inn* by the name, and you could feel an aura of spirituality on the grounds.

During the first year, in the mornings while guests were in the sunroom and we were in the hot kitchen with the door closed, I came up with the idea to have a small gift shop where guests, while sipping coffee and waiting on their scrumptious breakfast, could look around and possibly buy a gift for the babysitter, dog sitter, or simply something for their home. Pat and I registered with our tax number and became regulars at the gift shows in Atlanta. I always loved the gourmet section. We gorged on the latest culinary concoctions entrepreneurs created: chocolate popcorn, every flavor of fudge known to man, and many savory things, just to name a few out of hundreds. The scale reminded me to control myself. I found lots of delicacies, like pickled garlic (which still allows kissing), that my guests loved and purchased, along with many other things like relishes and jellies that became favorites for hors d'oeuvres.

On one trip, I bought small and delicate wooden music boxes because I liked the tunes. One day, a couple was checking out and I felt led to give them a music box, and I had no idea why I felt compelled to do so. Something inside me just said to do it. I said, "I have something for you," and returned with the tiny box.

When the wife opened it and heard the tune, she teared up with amazement and asked, "How did you know?"

When I asked what she meant, she replied, "This was my son's favorite hymn and he died in a car wreck last year."

We hugged and cried, and in that very moment I knew I was still filled with the Holy Spirit as I had been with Minnie and Marilyn. I thanked God for still trusting me to help others.

CHAPTER 21

The Rainbow and Roaming Elephants

The first year of owning and running the *Morning Star Inn* was difficult; especially being away from my sweet Pat except for weekends. I longed to hear his voice on the phone every day and that kept me going until our embrace on Friday afternoons. The car would be so loaded with food for the week that it took an hour to unload! We mingled with the guests while longing for our time alone . . . finally.

I decided that the first year we should stay open in the winter since the other inns closed and we would get all the business. Once more, little Miss naïve didn't know about the harshness of winters in Highlands yet, so the phone rarely rang. I remember one cold and rainy day; I was alone and missing Pat and feeling down and questioning if I could keep doing this. I was standing at my kitchen window watching the drizzling rain and prayed. I told God that if I was meant to continue this, I needed a sign. I was amazed that in my yard at that very moment in full sight of my window a bright rainbow in a glorious arch touched down in my yard. I had my answer.

Pat was able to sell his practice after three years of commuting, and we were thrilled. We were finally together again full time and loved this nice new pace. I still remember sitting on the edge of the bed talking to Pat on his birthday, March 27, and got tears in my eyes because he was now sixty years old, and I thought that was really old. How dumb was that? I told him we needed to travel and see the world while he was still able to get around. Remember, I'm thirteen years younger than him so I had no idea what sixty was like. We made the decision to close the inn in the winter and traveled extensively for three months until spring came, and I'm so glad we did.

We cruised on grand ships to ports in Europe and traveled to most of the towns in Australia. We went scuba diving in the Great Barrier Reef, snorkeled in Bali, visited most of the Caribbean islands, meandered through many Mexican towns and resorts, and went to Tuscany by train from Rome. But our favorite trip was an African safari at Londolozi Camp. After visiting Cape Town, which was amazing, we boarded a small plane in Johannesburg that was so tiny anyone taller than me (5 feet 4inches) had to bend over to get to their seat. The sky was a glorious blue, and after a short flight we landed on a small grassy airstrip in the middle of nowhere with a curious coyote watching us touch down. We were warmly greeted by our hosts and walked down a long path to our cabin and were pleasantly surprised. It was quite luxurious and done in Ralph Lauren style, with our own bar and a wonderful tile and spacious shower. The mahogany bed was canopied, and the colorful tiled floors were cool to the touch. There were just ten guests with our own gourmet chef. On the first evening, we gathered outside, and candles illuminated our surroundings as the darkness of night set in. The meal was fabulous as we engaged in conversation with other guests from other countries. We could hear sounds of lions in the distance and monkey hoots outside our windows.

Our daily routine consisted of embarking on open jeep rides at 5 a.m., tracking animals and witnessing their breakfast rituals in their natural habitats—no zoo here. Being so close to these majestic animals was surreal!

The jeep held six of us, and the man who served as the tracker sat in the lower front with rifle in hand in case we were attacked by an animal. We would look for footprints in the dirt and weeds that were flattened as an animal chose its path for the day. One morning, the tracker told the driver to make a turn saying, "Two lions went that way!"

Sure enough, we came upon them as the male had laid down in the shade for a quick nap. We observed until he got up and joined the female nearby for a "quickie" with an audience of eight. My face turned red but not from the African sun!

We would then return for an exquisite al fresco breakfast at 9 a.m. while mischievous little monkeys perched in the trees, awaiting a chance to swoop down and steal our bread or fruit with lightning speed. I loved their antics, which brought back memories of my pet monkey growing up. Maybe that's where my crazy personality comes from!

We would track again at 5 p.m. In the first afternoon, we saw elephants walk right past us, a leopard climbing gracefully to his treetop of choice, giraffes craning their long necks with curiosity, and zebras with different stripes than we see here in the US. We were told to sit very still and not talk, because that could cause the animals to feel threatened and possibly charge the Jeep. I was so afraid I might sneeze, causing the death of us all. The first day, the Jeep stopped in the middle of nowhere around 7 p.m. and we all looked at each other wondering what was next. The driver pulled out a tray of cheese, crackers, and an assortment of jerky and libations that we partook of while watching our first African sunset that was amazing in brilliant colors we had never experienced. That was our favorite trip ever. How could I have known it would be our last?

Being able to travel and see more of the world God created is a true gift. I often wonder why He created so many continents with such diverse cultures, different climates, and different races. That's another of life's mysteries.

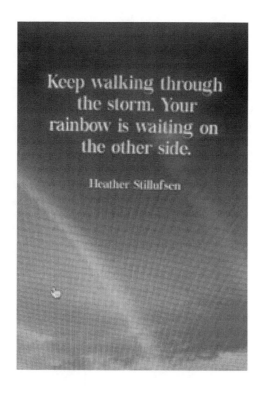

Keep walking through the storm. Your rainbow is waiting on the other side.

Heather Stillufsen

CHAPTER 22

Southern Living Magazine, Tiny Kitchen, and Big Hair

When we first opened the inn, I told one of our first guests who commented on the beauty of our place that one of my goals was to be in *Southern Living Magazine* one day. I had no idea how to make it happen but kept that goal in my mind. We had lovely grounds filled with flowers and shrubs, hammocks for napping, and a large front porch filled with wicker, geraniums, ferns, and a much-used swing. We created a tiny waterfall that fell over large boulders into a small water-filled pond showcasing water lilies and two large koi that I aptly named Forest and Gump after my favorite movie of all time! They proceeded to be very prolific!

A couple of years after opening the inn, one of our guests was a writer for *Victoria Magazine* and was in town to write about an artist in Cashiers, North Carolina—ten miles away. On our first evening of wine and hors d'oeuvres, she asked if I had ever considered doing cooking classes, and when I told her that I hadn't, she was adamant, stating how great our food was and what a great place the sunroom overlooking my perennial garden would be to have them. I sort of laughed and jokingly said, "If you put me in the magazine, I sure will do them!"

She informed me that they were looking for late fall and winter events to promote and if the editor liked my ideas, she would feature me.

That meant that after I got into bed at 11:00 I had to get my brain in creative mode, planning what to teach, how many students, and what to charge . . . quite a daunting task! This was before computers, so with a yellow legal pad and pen, and with a sleeping husband beside me, I planned cooking classes. The next morning, I sent the papers with the writer, doubtful I would ever hear from her again. A week later the editor called, and after many questions told me they wanted to add me to their list in the magazine.

I was excited but scared since this would be a first for me. Pat was delighted and thrilled, as well. I could hardly wait for the magazine to come out, and when it did my phone did not stop ringing. I had calls from all over the Southeast and added another class since the two I had initially planned filled up so quickly. One call I received was from a lady who wanted to enroll, and when I told her that all three classes were full, she asked if I would do them in the spring. I quickly thought to myself "why not?" and told her I would. When she asked that I take her info to stay in touch, she said to send it to *Southern Living Magazine* where she worked in the test kitchen! My heart was racing when I realized I had turned down *Southern Living Magazine*.

In November, my first students arrived, and you can imagine the prep Pat and I had to do. Not only did we have to feed them a gourmet breakfast followed by dishes to be washed, but then we had to prepare for the class. Our kitchen was tiny, with only one dishwasher and a small butcher block island for plating. The classes would be in the sunroom, which only had four small tables of four along with one chair we had added to accommodate our seventeen students. I had bought a high demonstration table with a gas burner, which became our "teaching" table. The classes would be two-day events. The first class was knife skills, which I felt most people didn't have and it really does save time in the kitchen. Garnishes and pretty plates would also be part of that class.

I put out knives, cutting boards, and bowls filled with tomatoes for roses, strawberries for fans, pears for mice on a cheese board, and lemons for twists. Pat and I wore chefs' coats I had ordered, and I really wanted him to be a part of the classes. He was such a trooper, and all the ladies loved him. I helped each student personally and guided their hands with band aids in full sight. We laughed a lot as some of their "roses" didn't bloom right and a few of the "mice" looked like rabbits, but everyone was excited and happy to be there, and after class they headed to Highlands to shop.

The dishes were insurmountable and stacked everywhere in the tiny kitchen. We would start the first load in the dishwasher and sit in the porch swing resting our feet and backs until we could load more dishes. These were such happy times and created sweet memories we would relive often.

The second day, the class was appetizers and hors d'oeuvres. Pat had concocted a hummus recipe that was a guest favorite. It had lots of garlic and lemon, but without the traditional tahini paste, so it was a lot less fattening. It was refreshing, and I had him demo it center stage. We passed warm pita bread for dipping and the students loved it. Other dishes included stuffed mushrooms with sausage and onions that gave off a heavenly scent that permeated the room and a divine strawberry dip with amaretto that we served with granny smith apples, just to name a few. Then more dishes and porch-swinging for us.

When the guests checked out on Sunday, we collapsed with relief but were thrilled that the classes were so successful. We made the decision to be an inn with a cooking school and added many more classes, even bringing in great chefs from five-star restaurants in Atlanta who were elated to come to the mountains, show off their skills, and make a little money!

The date in April was set for three of the ladies from the test kitchen at *Southern Living Magazine* to attend our classes. Needless to say, we were nervous wrecks. The pressure was on! The ladies arrived and were so gracious and loved our classes and my Pat. We sat around in our pajamas and drank wine and laughed a lot. We did our two original classes, and they were impressed. When they left on Sunday, we exchanged hugs, and they said they were going to talk to their editor about featuring our inn. I anxiously awaited and soon after received a call from the editor saying he wanted to send a writer and photographer to interview us. They did a two-page story with photos of the inn and Pat and me in our beloved swing. It was a great photo of Pat, but I hated my big hair!

This was a dream that became a reality and an example of envisioning what you want and letting your subconscious lead you there. I had no clue how to do a cooking class but researched and let my knowledge take over letting my fear dissipate. Always dream big and don't let fear stop you.

CHAPTER 23

Chocolate Mice and White Painted Corks

On December 16, 2001, it was our seventh year of running the inn. I was at a friend's house learning to make the chocolate "mice" that she had brought to a garden club event, and I was anxious to make them myself. Before I could get the first "tail" on the body, I received a call saying Mama had been in a car wreck in Athens, Georgia, two hours away. Fear went through me, and I called Pat and told him to pack a bag quickly. She was traveling with two of my aunts and seated on the passenger side of the car. They were going from Macon to Athens to see another aunt, and they could have aptly been the real Golden Girls. It was cold outside and warm in the car, and my Aunt Ida fell asleep at the wheel and the car slammed into the back of an eighteen-wheeler. Police cars guided the ambulances and helicopter that was subsequently summoned. My Aunt Violet, who had been sitting in the back seat, was airlifted to Augusta Medical Center, and Mama and my other aunt went by ambulance to St. Mary's Hospital in Athens.

We sped our way to see these precious family members and made the two-hour trip in an hour and a half. Mama had been admitted with a fractured pelvis and a gash on her head that required twenty stitches. My Aunt Ida had numerous injuries and it was the first time in her seventy-something years that anyone in the family learned that she only had one kidney. She would remain on dialysis for the rest of her life. Pat and I walked briskly down the hall, and upon entering Mama's room saw her with a bandage on her forehead and her leg suspended in the air by a metal contraption. A sense of insecurity filled me, seeing this strong woman weakened and in this shape. She was still in pain, and as I was looking at her wounds, she got a phone call and her eyes filled with tears, having been told that my Aunt Violet didn't survive. It was a terrible day, and Mama was in pain both physically and emotionally.

When she was released from St. Mary's, she was sent to a rehab center in Macon for intermittent care. It was Christmas Day, and I called the facility to talk with her. She was very unhappy and said, "Can you believe they have me in diapers?"

As soon as I ate lunch, I headed to Macon to console her. Since she lived alone, I knew Pat and I needed to get a place in Macon so I could care for her when she was allowed to go home. As it turned out she was confined to a wheelchair for six weeks and her house was not handicapped accessible, so we rented a house owned by one of my friends for the first month. Mama would ring a bell in the night when she needed to go to the bathroom, and I would sleepwalk to tend to her needs. I did my best to restrict her liquids at dinner knowing the little bell was exhausting me. Ironically, nowadays I limit my own liquids at night, so I don't have to pee constantly.

Pat had suffered from back pain for as long as I had known him, and it was getting worse. He was going to require surgery to get better, and I knew what I needed to do. I proceeded to tell Pat that we needed to close the inn and get a place in Macon temporarily so I could tend to both him and my mother. One of my best friends was a realtor and found us a lovely townhome in an area with a lake. Mama loved to fish more than anybody I knew, and when she was able, I could take her fishing as much as she wanted. We also knew good doctors in Macon who could do Pat's surgery, so we bought the townhome. We reconnected with some old friends and were near a Methodist church we learned to love. It was smaller than the one we previously attended, Mulberry Methodist located downtown, but Martha Bowman Church was closer to our home. It was so good to be back in church since we were always checking people out on Sunday mornings at the inn and couldn't attend one. This continued for a year until I knew it was time to return to Highlands, which I now considered home.

Mama was finally able to walk again, and we spent many hours sitting on the bank of the lake. The sun was warm, and birds flew overhead. She painted her corks white, hoping to see them better. She was so happy, except that her macular degeneration had progressed, so I would sit close by and tell her when the cork was bobbing. Some days were better than others as far as our abundant "catch," but just having hours together made it worth every sunburn I encountered. Those were special days for us that I will always cherish. Again, I know God's hand was there to reunite us.

*Family is so important, and I know as you grow older with our own kids and grandkids or grand dogs, time is limited for your parents. But remember, they were the giver of your life and never expected to have the health issues that will surely come their way. Whether just physical or mental as well, there is depression knowing they can't do the things they once could and have aches and pains they never experienced before, limiting their mobility. They aren't as sharp as they once were, and memory loss is inevitable. Make time and be kind . . . they can't change it. You will never regret being there for them, and once it's over you can't go back. I often think of things I wish I had asked Mama or my brother but didn't have the insight to do so before they passed away. My questions will remain unanswered.

CHAPTER 24

The Surprising Circle of Life . . . Connecting the Dots

After closing the inn, I realized that making it our home for two years would be more profitable for us than trying to sell it as a business. Even though the business had been successful, the capital gain tax when we sold it would be huge since real estate values in Highlands continued to rise. We were worth 2.5 times more than our original investment, and the tax consequences would be enormous. We decided to live in our lovely place and have the run of the house for the first time ever, instead of living downstairs with the tiny bedroom and bath. We enjoyed having the largest bedroom and the great room with the large wood-burning fireplace and private porch and swing access whenever we wanted. The sunroom became a haven for reading or having our guests for dinner.

I recall the sense of freedom after seven years of tending to everyone else, and now it was just Pat and me. The kids, who all lived out of town, loved to come and visit, mastering the hiking trails nearby. We gathered for Christmas with an enormous tree in the great room and themed trees in each bedroom. Luckily, we had a huge attic to store decorations, and at some point, a local person told me it was haunted. Well, it must have been a friendly ghost because I was never frightened going up there. It was just a lovely home when we lived in it, ghost included!

We continued to travel and one of our favorite places was San Miquel de Allende, Mexico. So many people from Highlands would make it their destination of choice every January or February to escape the cold winters we had come to know. I decided we should explore it and made a reservation for the following February. It sounded delightful, and I reserved a house from their local newspaper, *The Attencion*. We flew from Atlanta to Leon, Mexico, neither of us knew any Spanish except for the basics, including hola, buenos dias, buenas noches, el bano (which was a must!), and a few other random words and phrases.

We arrived around 9 p.m. over-laden with luggage (after all, this was a month in a climate I was unfamiliar with) and someone in Highlands had told me there would be Mercedes buses to take us on the hour and a half journey to San Miquel. There were no buses to be found. All I saw were small cars, and many used as taxis. I tried to talk to someone at an office there and she finally comprehended what I said enough to get us a taxi, telling him where we were headed. Surprisingly, the diminutive taxi driver lifted all our bags easily and secured them on top of his small car with rope. Pat and I looked at each other with wonder and off we went through the dark countryside to parts unknown. We commented later that this was the perfect opportunity to be kidnapped and never be heard from again. We sat in silence most of the way, being tired and hungry. The driver didn't speak English and we were at his mercy.

When we finally saw lights approaching in what appeared to be a town, the little man rolled down the window, asking where Huertas Street was, which was our destination for the next month. When we arrived, there were two massive yellow doors protecting the home. I pushed the button and was delighted to hear the homeowner's voice speaking in English, saying that he was there to meet us and familiarize us with the home. The doors opened to reveal the most beautiful mansion, with grounds filled with flowers and a small guest house (casita) in the back. I couldn't wait for the morning light to take it all in!

Meanwhile, the owner helped us up the grand staircase with our luggage to a beautiful bedroom and large bath. We were in heaven. We did ask if there was some place to get food, as we were starving. He tried to tell us a street to find nearby with a restaurant that served late on the weekends. Pat was pretty good with directions, but not that night. We wound up in an area where we heard sounds of a mariachi band with saloon doors inviting us in. We loved the Mexican tile and look of the place and sat at a small table for two. There were a few others in the bar, and we couldn't wait to try a "real" margarita, which has always been my drink of choice since age twenty-one, and the smiling waitress brought chips and salsa and took our order.

The first sip of my drink was felt down to my toes, but it was so good, and I was thirsty, and jet lagged. Pat loved his too but was really a scotch drinker. We only had snack food, and after finishing our drink, the waitress brought two more margaritas, complements of the table nearby. We nodded and smiled, thinking how nice, but we just wanted to get to our home and go to bed, so we drank them quickly and headed out the door. We both looked at each other as if to say, "I have no clue where we are or how to find the house!"

We were jet-lagged, intoxicated, it was midnight in Mexico with hardly anyone on the streets, and we didn't know enough Spanish to even ask someone directions. Luckily, my ability to backtrack kicked in and we staggered on the streets until we found the mustard-colored doors. We managed to crawl up the stone stairs to the bedroom, but I immediately knew I had to get to the porcelain bowl to lose what I had just ingested. When I tried to stand up and walk to the bedroom, where Pat had passed out on the bed, my mind said move forward and my body kept backing up. All I could do was sleep on the cool tile floor until morning broke.

We had a maid, a gardener, and a cook. The impeccable grounds of green grass and bougainvillea that draped every visible space and a fountain frequented by doves made me think this must be what heaven is like. The warmth of the sun's rays and a light sweater were all we needed to explore the shops and restaurants. We could feel the love these people had for their families, and the large church (the Parroquia) was filled with love and a spirit of unification. Little children were in the streets selling Chiclets and we always felt sorry that parents had to send the little ones out to sell to try and make ends meet. Many times, I would buy all they had so they could go home, but looking back that probably encouraged the parents to make them sell more.

The smells of street corn permeated the air, but I was afraid my stomach might not tolerate it. Vendors were always selling balloons with various faces of cats and cartoon-looking characters. The town square was a great respite from walking the cobblestoned streets and offered many benches to "take a load off" and people watch. The brilliant colors of the surrounding flowers, the vibrant colors of the homes, the energy of the hard-working people and love for their families, where less is fine, and a sense of spirituality, make this a special place on Earth, and we would return many times.

In San Miguel, one American tradition became gathering on rooftop terraces to watch the gorgeous sunsets with delightful cocktail parties. A lady from Memphis, Tennessee, realized how this town had become a mecca for Americans and moved there to start a rental company, connecting travelers with these gorgeous homes. We attended as many as possible while there over the years and enjoyed meeting people from all over the country who shared our excitement of being there.

Another tradition for American tourists was a tour of homes on Sundays. We would meet at the local library (the Biblioteca), buy a ticket, board a much-used school bus, and tour magnificent homes, and the proceeds would benefit the local libraries. We were in awe of the beauty of these authentic Mexican homes with impeccable grounds. On one of our tours, we entered and were greeted by a docent and all of us were shocked at the same time to see Chip Wilson, the innkeeper from Valle Crucis, who was instrumental in our road to innkeeping! She revealed that she had sold her inn, moved to San Miquel, and had remarried. She invited us to dinner and their place was gorgeous, filling me with envy. They had purchased a home right outside of town and basically gutted it, maintaining the local flavor. The craftsmen were amazing with their tile and stonework and the home turned out to be magnificent.

It was so good to reconnect. Pat and Jim were similar in their gentle natures and ability to allow us women to "rule the roost," knowing we had proven our ability to do so. By this time, I had become a realtor (next chapter), and we stayed in touch, and to my surprise, about a year later, Chip called and said they had sold their home in Mexico and bought a home in Fairhope, Alabama, but were considering a second home in Highlands. I was thrilled and delighted to be their broker . . . more on that later.

Chip had found a log home that intrigued her on the internet, and they made the trip to Highlands to see it. It was built by Tommy Chambers, known for his craftsmanship in designing and building log homes. I met Chip and Jim there, and upon entering observed a tiny great room with a large wood burning fireplace and a small table and two chairs for dining, a kitchen without room for a dishwasher, and a small, tiled bath on the main floor. Upstairs was a bedroom with just enough room for a bed and tiny dresser, and an open loft overlooking the bedroom. A Hobbit house came to mind. The thought of coming down the staircase at night to pee would have ruled it out for me. Chip loved it and the grounds were perfect for gardening and Jim, an avid gardener, saw great potential there.

They asked me to write the offer and it became their second home. We were asked to dinner and ate outside among the flowering plants and shrubs and had a great meal with wine flowing and the katydids serenading us as twilight came. Jim was later diagnosed with bone cancer, and their world changed in an instant. He was treated with various drugs but died months later. We were saddened, as Pat and Jim had become good friends, and the world had lost a nice man.

Within a year of Jim's passing, Chip decided to move to Highlands full time, and we found a condo in a fifty-five-plus community that she gutted and with her eye for design made an incredible home. We still have dinner and talk about the wonderful husbands we had and how ironic we both had inns, loved San Miquel where we reconnected, and both wound up living in Highlands, North Carolina. This would complete a circle of different people's roles in my life, with others I will reveal later.

*There is a mystery and sense of wonder when people enter your life, stay for a while, leave for a while, and re-enter. Is it fate that the story hasn't ended yet? Is there still a lesson to be learned, moments to share, or just a sense of sharing a special time in your lives together? That is one of life's unsolved mysteries.

CHAPTER 25

My Last Fork in the Road that Led the Path to a Silver Spoon

A year passed by quickly as Mama recuperated from the car accident, and I knew it was time to return to Highlands. The year was 2003. Then the question for me was what to do workwise. We had sold the inn and I had too much drive and energy to do nothing. I had a few friends in real estate, and after giving it some thought I decided to go to real estate school. After all, I loved houses and decorating, and many of our inn guests came to town searching for property. It seemed like a good fit. Little did I know the lion's den I was entering. I thought I would work when I wanted to, and I would be in control of my hours. How naïve was I?

Pat and I drove to Asheville, North Carolina, every weekend for a month and made the most of it, seeking the best restaurants after class. The studying was intense since I was in an accelerated class, but Pat was always so supportive of anything I wanted to do. Upon completion of the course, the test by the North Carolina Real Estate Commission was given on a computer at a testing center, and I was nervous and felt the questions to be somewhat tricky. When the screen read "You passed," I was shocked but thrilled.

I put my license in the Highlands office owned by the number one independent firm in Atlanta, which at that time sold over three billion dollars a year. This was a small office, with seven desks and brokers. I was gung-ho to go, and my first two listings were from acquaintances who could feel my energy and drive to be successful. Another client was a friend from Macon who was building a development in Highlands. I was excited, and ironically, my first sale occurred because of my working late and from a couple wandering in from the ice cream parlor next door. The house they bought was not one I would have wanted, but I learned early on to always make it about them, and not me. That holds true to this day.

When I got my first commission check, I was amazed to make $8,000, and Pat was so proud. The broker-in-charge at that time was not very friendly and resented the brokers from the Atlanta parent company who would stop in to use our fax or copy machine. She said they never sent us referrals, but later I realized that wasn't true. She was not polished and cussed like a sailor . . . so different from Buckhead, Atlanta brokers! Buckhead was where the parent company was located and the affluent reside there. Three other offices were in that vicinity, as well. After six months, and with Christmas approaching, she learned she wasn't getting a Christmas bonus and so turned in her resignation. The Atlanta folks and our team were stunned. After one week of the two-week resignation period, she took the computer that wasn't hers and took a job as broker-in-charge (BIC) with a competitor.

In July of that year Pat and I were in the Bahamas, never having been there before. One afternoon, after scorching my lily-white skin beachside, I received a phone call from Lewis, the president of the major real estate firm in Atlanta. I was shocked, having never met him, and he asked if when we flew into Atlanta, we could set up a meeting. I agreed, not understanding the reason, and we met in a hotel lobby. He was tall and slender and dressed in a business suit on a Sunday. His CFO was beside him. We greeted each other and took our seats, Pat by my side. The two men were similar in nature, being kind Southern gentlemen, and seemed to connect with us immediately.

The dilemma of the day was whether to keep the Highlands office going, since it had not been successful in eight years. There were reasons for that, the main one being that the first BIC they sent from Atlanta made the comment, "We are here to show these rednecks how to sell real estate."

The word spread and the other firms boycotted, defiant that they would keep the Buckhead group from succeeding in this town. That lady who was the original BIC died suddenly after about a year, and the other BICs were never the right fit so the firm didn't succeed or make a profit, as it should have.

The president asked me my thoughts on the Highlands office, and I asked, "good news or bad news first?"

He sort of laughed, and I proceeded. I told how the office started on the wrong foot, with the Buckhead BIC insulting locals. I've learned, over the years, that there is a fine line that must be followed with admiration and respect for all.

The locals are genuine, good people who saw their town change with what they felt was an invasion by affluent people wanting to take over. That is still the perception to date, but it has been generally accepted seeing improvements to the town that would otherwise have not been possible. I told the president that there should be no reason why we couldn't be in the top three consistently, but currently were always number six or seven. I talked about lack of marketing and community involvement, showing we really did care about the town. He said to give him forty-eight hours to make a decision, and I asked that he cut it to twenty-four since one of our brokers was in Paris and wanted to know if he had a desk to come back to when he returned. He laughed and left.

Pat and I went to dinner, and when we returned to the room, I received a call from the president who said, "I want to officially offer you the position of broker-in-charge of the Highlands office."

I was stunned, and replied, "I don't even have my broker's license yet, I'm just an agent!"

At that time, you had to go back to school to get a broker's license. He answered with, "We will take care of that. There is something I see in you, and I know you can do this."

Needless to say, I was shocked and proceeded to tell him that I would have to think about it and discuss it with Pat, knowing my life would change yet again. Pat and I discussed it that evening and again the next morning. He thought it was a great opportunity and an honor to be asked. I was reluctant, knowing this would be a full-time job, and I hardly even knew how to use a computer!

My thoughts of working only when I wanted to would become a thing of the past if I stepped into this position, but something inside nudged me to accept the offer, so I called the president and accepted, not knowing the dark road that lay ahead. The brokers I had been working with did not understand how a beginner to the business of real estate could all of a sudden be the one they would answer to. Neither did I, really. There was tension and resentment that we struggled through, since now I was in the "big" office. My only objective was to meet a goal, and I always felt a responsibility to Lewis who believed in me even more than I knew.

I remember the long hours involved, and one night within the first week I was sitting at my computer at the office writing ads for the next real estate magazine with the deadline being the next day. I had never really used Microsoft Word much, and when I thought I was finished at 9:30 that night, I forgot to hit save, and all my creativity in writing the ads was for naught because they disappeared. I sat and cried, and then drove my weary self home, feeling defeated. Pat held me, assuring me it was fine. The next day when Luke, the publisher of The Buyers Guide Magazine came by to pick up the new ads I told him what happened, telling him just to run the same ads as the previous month! I finally got the hang of it and life went on.

I learned a lot about management the hard way. I learned that no matter how hard you try, not all people will like you, and there will always be resentment. I was required to have office meetings every Tuesday, and one guy, who I had been friends with for twenty years, totally ignored me and stayed on eBay the whole time. I later had to ask him to leave, and I missed our friendship and that of his wife for many years.

I think this is a classic example of the importance of having the support of a loving spouse or partner. If I had not had Pat to cheer me on, I probably would not have taken on this responsibility that led to my profound success. So, the importance of being in a good relationship offers strength and confidence you might not otherwise acquire. One good decision in life leads to other good decisions in life. Plan yours accordingly.

CHAPTER 26

Friends Come and Go but Real Ones Stay Forever

Friends play such an important part in all our lives, whether we are married or alone. The word friend is defined in the dictionary as: "a person whom one knows and with whom one has a bond of mutual affection, typically exclusive of sexual or family relations." That really does sum up my belief in friendship, with the keyword being "mutual."

I remember having many friends in grammar school, but there were a few that I had affection for and would now only be defined as mere acquaintances. We had fun at recess, talking about boys and laughing, and it was on the schoolyard I learned about sex from a ten-year-old girl who described it with enough graphic details that fear took over and I knew I would NEVER do such a thing. I simply was terrified that someone else's body part could fit in mine . . . . surely that wasn't true!! Eventually that changed, of course!

One good friend's name was Brenda and we had similar home life situations. We would have sleepovers and continued our antics in high school with some of our other friends. Our high school in Macon, Miller High, was an all-girls school, so our only exposure to boys was at parties. I was always the designated driver because, with my church upbringing, I felt it was wrong to drink until I was officially twenty-one, but I didn't judge others. After all, I'm a Methodist . . . LOL! Later in life, Brenda married the wrong guy, had two children, divorced, then married a doctor with stepchildren. We still visit and sometimes travel together. Memories return and we laugh at some and are sad with others.

When I was divorced in 1984, my best friend, Terri, (Sunday school brunette)—who I had known from church since our kids were little—and I would travel together, and she was so funny! She drove one of those large Bonneville's and drove like a little old lady and we were in our thirties! Her ex-husband was not a good guy and so our discussions were how to find the "right man" this time! She liked her Jack Daniels and once my date had to leave me to go and pull her car from a ditch! She eventually married an older man who died on Christmas Day, and I always told her I would be there when Charlie died because his stepchildren were so mean to her. I left Christmas afternoon and was there by her side through the funeral.

She is now remarried and living in a small town in North Carolina and is very happy. She is the kind of friend even though we don't see each other often, the sound of her voice brings back good memories and the love that brought us together with so many heartaches as single moms but also the funny escapades we shared over the years.

One of my current best friends in Highlands is a little older than I am, and we became acquainted when I was asked to list her house for sale. My Pat had already passed away and we both are so sorry they never met. The more she and I were around each other, the more we connected. In some ways, she reminded me of my mother with her independent ways and determination to do things for herself. She would crawl under the house on her belly to check a sewer line, and no amount of money could make me do that. She is a big animal lover, and both of us are into supporting rescues and our local Humane Society that is a no-kill-shelter. She has an impish side, as do I. We are sort of the "Lucy and Ethel" of Highlands. We both also love to help others and give back to the community.

When she and I had been friends for about two years and shared details of our lives, I mentioned how therapy had changed my life and that I had lost touch with the therapist because he moved to Atlanta. She shared her years of having therapy with a great therapist in Atlanta, and when she said his name, it was my therapist!! What are the odds? And then she said he and his partner had a second home in Highlands! I had often longed to see him and thank him for my new life he helped create. We were at the opening night of our new performing arts center in Highlands two years ago and as she and I were trying to find our seats, I heard her say, "Hey Jim!"

I looked up, and of course would not have recognized him after forty years, but had to hug him and whispered, "Thank you for changing my life."

His reply was, "I didn't change your life, WE changed your life together," and I knew he was right.

In our various stages in life, we choose friends with similar interests and situations. As we mature, we may change our outlook in life, and perhaps our friend doesn't change, creating a drift. Friends may become jealous if you have a life change, whether a divorce, job promotion, or simply a gain in confidence they can't relate to.

Betrayal is likely and is hard to predict. Choose wisely who you are vulnerable with because they may not be a true friend. It's like giving them the password to your computer. As we have learned as we have gotten older people say disparaging things about us to make themselves look better. In the end others will see them for who they really are. Don't be pulled down to their level and share in their misery.

*A dear friend may move to another state that makes it more difficult to stay in touch. But one thing I know is those you really connect with in heart and soul are always there and have your back. You can call day or night and it all rushes back in love and spirit. Nourish those connections, because one day you will need them, and they will need you.

CHAPTER 27

I Jumped This Hurdle in a Girdle and it Almost Squeezed the Life Out of Me

I continued my role as BIC for seven years and did take us to a consistent number one, two, or three in market share in Highlands, having mended relationships with local firms and Atlanta brokers who now felt welcome in our office. It was a daunting task, but I was determined to achieve my goal and keep my promise to the president. Pat met me every day for lunch and was very patient the many times I was delayed. Many buyers wanted to work with me since I was the BIC, and some of my other brokers felt I was "stealing" their business. I was working six days a week and usually left about 6:30, at which time Pat and I went to dine in town.

My skin became thicker, and I learned that success breeds jealousy by others who are either insecure or refuse to work as hard as they should but want what you have. I always wanted everyone to like me, and perhaps those feelings of being rejected by the high school girls for not being from a prominent family resurfaced. One day I realized I was now the prominent one and no longer needed anyone's affirmation. I was now in control of my life and its destination was up to me.

When Pat had some serious health problems in 2011, I did some soul-searching and realized we needed to enjoy our time together and made the decision to give up my position as a full-time real estate broker in charge. The year before, the Atlanta firm sold to Warren Buffet's Home Services. The new corporation decided any out-of-town offices must be franchised—something I never wanted—but when the president offered to give it to me, I didn't refuse. I only had to pay for the furniture and equipment.

I was willing to just close the door, but when I told one of my brokers, she said she had a friend she thought would take it. My thought was that it would be great in that my brokers would still have a place to work and wouldn't have to change firms, and I could work only when I felt like it. I met this woman and didn't really feel a connection, but thought it was our only solution. I had to take her to Atlanta to meet the president for approval, having explained Pat's diagnosis and my need to do this. He approved, and her friend who put us together would be the BIC, since she, the new owner, only had six months of experience as a broker and the rule was you must have two years of full-time experience to declare yourself as broker-in-charge.

Immediately, we got off to a bad start as she informed us at the first sales meeting she now conducted that we were to have no headshots in our ads. She thought they were "cheesy." I explained how important it was to be marketing ourselves, but she didn't back down until a few others objected. I realized that she did not like me and was anxious to take control, all the while I was trying to keep things going at home and at work. My commitment to the president was always on my mind.

Three weeks after taking over, she fired her friend who recommended her and who was to become the BIC so I could relinquish that role. Then I was stuck again, and she said I needed to do it until she could find a replacement. She came into the office less and less as the days went by. I kept us going as before, trying to cut my hours to spend time with Pat.

One day, I came in on a Thursday and the owner asked me how to fill out the form for the Georgia license for the firm, since the BIC had to be licensed in both states. I could see she was filling out the form from the North Carolina Real Estate Commission to make herself the BIC. When I reminded her that she didn't have two years of experience as a full-time broker, she replied, "I know but I'm doing it anyway."

I cringed, knowing if I allowed that we would all be working illegally in the firm. I mentioned it to two brokers in my firm and told them we couldn't work under her, knowing we were in an illegal situation. I left that day wondering how we would handle this.

On the following rainy Saturday morning, I walked into my office to pick up a few things for an open house I was doing at a condo development I represented. She walked into my office, shutting the door behind her. She sat down and told me I was fired. I was shocked and asked why she would fire me, the number one salesperson and BIC? She just replied, "Get the F . . . out of my office. Get your things and get out!"

I knew then that by telling our brokers we would be working illegally under her, she became outraged. I told her there was so much anger right now that I was going to my open house, and we could talk when I returned. She once again said, "Get the F . . . out of my office."

I left, and when I returned two hours later my computer was gone. My laptop had crashed so I had no way to work. I told her I needed my computer because I was writing an offer, and she said it belonged to her. It had all my personal files on there and she now had access to them. I never saw the computer again. I had called Pat to tell him of my situation, and once he arrived at the office, I told him we had to go to Best Buy, an hour and a half away, to get my laptop fixed. We left and talked about this in the car, trying to figure out how to handle it. I had officially been fired.

I called the new president of the parent company in Atlanta to inform him of the situation and basically was told that when I gave her the franchise, they were no longer in control of our office. She was free to hire and fire, as she chose to do. I was devastated and Best Buy said it would be three days before they could restore my laptop.

We drove back to the office so I could get my personal things and files, and when I put my key in the door realized the locks had been changed. I tried calling the owner and got a voicemail and left a message telling her I needed my things. I was now living in hell and felt helpless. There was no one to talk to except my sweet Pat and my inner self. Over the weekend I had a decision to make. Did I just let it all go and retire from real estate or forge ahead building on my reputation and the obligation I felt to my clients and my brokers? Should I let a mean-spirited person destroy what I had achieved? Here was the tallest hurdle of my career and it had created chaos unlike any I had ever experienced. There would be shock and awe in my little Hallmark town, and I had a major decision to make.

On Monday afternoon, I decided to go full speed ahead and have my own firm. I didn't have an office but knew I could work out of the model unit at Town Place, the condominium complex

I was representing, but to do that I needed a logo and signs. I called my friend Katy, who had worked at the local newspaper and did our ads, and explained the situation and that I needed a logo ASAP! Within two hours, she sent me the logo I still use today. I talked with our sign guy, who was always so nice, and told him I needed signs fast and that Katy would send him the logo. They both rallied, and on that Friday, I picked up my beautiful signs. To everyone's amazement they were seen all over town that weekend. Most people in town had no idea what had transpired. Those who did were totally shocked that she would fire her number one producer and BIC.

When I explained to my sellers what had happened, ninety percent of them withdrew from the brokerage that I had been employed with and listed with me. Most were outraged and shocked and expressed loyalty to me. I was so thankful for how things fell into place. I had left messages with the CEO of the parent company in Atlanta all week that I needed my files and keys to my listings. I was ignored until I called one last time, the moment I picked up my signs, and told his voicemail that I still didn't have my files and keys and felt "raped" by those involved.

Within thirty minutes the vindictive owner called to say the secretary would deliver them to the model unit (my office) within an hour. She arrived with two boxes. One had mixed papers dumped out of files and the other had all the keys, but she had removed all the key tags! Evil does exist, and I had witnessed it once more. Her business survived for two years without me and then closed.

Pat Allen Realty Group resulted from this, and I was a one-person show until I called a broker I knew who had not worked in a while. She came to work with me, but that didn't last long once I realized we were not compatible. After hearing my dilemma and having worked for the same parent company in Atlanta for seven years, my daughter Julie, decided to move to Highlands and join my firm and we became partners. We moved into a quaint building on Dillard Road that had a cute apartment in the back with a fireplace, loft bedroom, bath, and full kitchen. She lived there for four years until she bought her own place that would turn out to be a great investment. Julie always wondered why her little dog, Lucy, was always nervous at night and barked a lot. Years later we bought cameras that showed the backyard to be an impromptu animal sanctuary with bears, raccoons, and cats who loved to hang out there.

We were a great team because Julie is very detailed- unlike me whose mind is in constant chaos with new ideas! We added many new and great brokers, and our business grew quickly. We were always leaders, winning top awards. Being ethical, honest, and always putting our clients' needs first led to our success.

In my ten years as Pat Allen Realty Group, I hired many new brokers who remain faithful to this day. Two years ago, I was approached by Allen Tate Realtors out of Charlotte, North Carolina, and we started negotiations for them to purchase Pat Allen Realty Group. They are the largest independent firm in the country and are number one in sales in the country, including both Carolinas. They remind me of the original brokerage I worked for in Atlanta, and the respectable president who hired me. Pat Riley, CEO, is a kind southern gentleman who always takes the "high road," as I was always advised to do. I love the entire company and was so honored that they chose my firm to be a part of them.

I also find it ironic that both firms, the largest independent one in Atlanta, and Howard Hanna (that Allen Tate is affiliated with) were marked for success due to the strong leadership of women: Mrs. Emmaline Norman, who created Atlanta's first real estate firm in 1930 and Helen Hanna Casey, the iconic Chief Executive Officer of Howard Hanna Real Estate, the third largest real estate company in the United States and the largest one that is privately owned. Both were driven, determined, and beat the odds in a man's industry that paid off and I'm fortunate to have been a small fragment of their achievements in the industry.

And looking back, the hell I went through that brought me to my knees was the highest hurdle I jumped with my short legs and with my mind filled with insecurities. But the subsequent decision to start my own firm was worth it and led to my success. Had I not jumped, my life would have been totally different, and I would not be writing this book. For you younger readers who probably don't know what a girdle is, just think very tight Spanx.

The biggest decisions in life give us two choices: stay in our comfort zone where we feel no discomfort and are stuck in the status quo or muster every bit of courage we have and jump the hurdle. You will be amazed at what the other side has to offer.

CHAPTER 28

The Beginning of the End and a Dream I'll Never Forget

When I married my sweet Pat, I was thirty-seven years old, and he was forty-nine. Many were skeptical that the marriage would work. He loved scotch and soda and would tend to overindulge at times. I would learn that he was rather shy and was much more social when drinking. He also drank to hide the pain of being divorced with three children he had little contact with. His ex-wife lived in Atlanta, and the girls rarely came to visit. His son came to live with him in Macon to finish his senior year of high school until he left for college.

Pat grew up in Jackson, Mississippi, and went to dental school at the University of Tennessee in Memphis. After graduating, he joined the Air Force, where he was an officer and was stationed for four years in Aviano, Italy. It was there that he learned to ski and drink wine. After two years of practicing general dentistry, he decided to become an oral surgeon, with his fellowship being in Rochester, Minnesota, at the Mayo Clinic. He was recruited to join another oral surgeon in Macon, Georgia, as a partner.

That is how he arrived in Macon, where we eventually met after his divorce.

If there is such a thing, we had the perfect marriage for thirty-three years. We were best friends, and I knew without any doubt that we were meant to share our lives together. We had ups and downs with his kids, and I tried hard to make us a family, but blended families are never easy. There is always jealousy and resentment, but we endured because of our great love.

On Christmas Eve 2011, my life was about to change forever. Julie and her husband were visiting us in Highlands. We were all chatting, by the fireplace and with the enormous tree with lights that cast a warm glow throughout the large great room, and I suggested Pat make his wonderful key lime martinis. As I glanced at him walking, I noticed that he had a slight shuffle I had never seen before. He was gone longer than it should have taken so I went to check on him. He was standing at the bar with a confused look on his face and said, "I don't remember how to make them," even though he made them so often. My heart sank, and I knew deep down that where we were headed was not good.

When we saw a doctor after Christmas, they determined his blood pressure was very high, and when he was asked a few questions, Pat couldn't answer them all correctly. He was referred to a young neurologist who, looking back, was rather incompetent. His MRI machine was in the parking lot, and after several visits, the doctor called me at my office to say it was Alzheimer's. I went numb, knowing the horror of that disease. He basically said to go and live life and enjoy as many days as we could.

I cried for days, hiding it from Pat, not telling him what the doctor said. I wanted a second opinion. It took weeks, but

I wanted him to see the head of neurology at Mayo Clinic. We finally secured an appointment, and I was anxious and afraid of the diagnosis. After examining him and seeing the MRI, he determined it to be hydrocephalus, which is there when you're born but for some people is dormant until they are older.

This means that a small amount of spinal fluid leaks into your brain on a constant basis and interferes with mental acuity. The doctor said typically he would put a shunt in to reroute the fluid into the stomach, but with Pat's history of high blood pressure and type 2 diabetes, the risk was too great. We were told it could be years before it was debilitating, and so for five years we managed, but mentally the changes were obvious, and his balance was affected. Pat started to fall, and Julie and I were really concerned for his safety. We had to make a decision and it was the hardest I've ever had to make. Julie, my daughter, who had been an occupational therapist at all three Mayo Clinics, found an excellent memory care facility in Athens, where she also had a condo. We went to see it and it was lovely. Since they had only one opening, we needed to secure it quickly. Pat looked around and thought it was very nice, but I don't think he comprehended that it was about to become his home. We bought furniture and set up his room, including his recliner. I remember him saying, "This is a nice hotel room."

I stayed with him the first night, but the administrator said they discouraged that very often so he could adjust to his new home. Looking back, I wish I had stayed there more.

Athens is a two-hour drive from Highlands, and I would visit two to three days a week. He always begged me not to leave, and I cried on the way home. The first day when I came home from leaving him, I had never felt so alone. The house was so empty, and my mind couldn't accept he would not return; that the meals we shared, the quiet moments reading, the movies we watched, the laughter we shared, and the bed where we held each other were gone and would only be memories. I think maybe I went into post-traumatic stress disorder. I was depressed and my behavior was sometimes weird, just trying to exist in a life of uncertainty.

Pat and I would talk every day and he pleaded for me to come and get him. I was so tempted but knew he would keep falling and might wander off. We lived upstairs, and if he fell down the stairs it would kill him. I buried myself in my work. Pat and I were inseparable, having had breakfast, lunch, and dinner together every day for thirty-two years. His social life was going to dinner at one of Highland's restaurants every night. Everyone loved him, and I honestly don't think he had an enemy in this world. The sadness we both felt was overwhelming, but there was no good answer.

After a few months in that facility, Julie and I went to visit on a Sunday. The nurse had called to tell me he had been throwing up and a stomach virus was going around, and I shouldn't come for several days. When we did arrive and walked in, he was pale and looked terrible. Julie took his pulse and immediately said, "We are going to the hospital ER!"

He was in atrial fibrillation (A Fib), which is an irregular and often very rapid heart rhythm and was admitted for several days.

We took turns staying with him at night, and Julie recalls a special night when they talked about life, and she felt an extra closeness to him. They had always had a bond, but it seemed that night they could express it. When it was time to be discharged, he was sent to a rehab facility in Athens for improving balance and walking. I would visit and we would sit with the other patients and share stories. It was a happier time for a while, adjusting to rehab instead of a memory care unit.

Then another decision had to be made when he was being released from there. I wanted him back in an assisted living facility in Highlands, and there was a room available for him. I was thrilled that I would just have to drive a couple of miles to see him every day. I got to take him to restaurants he loved, and everyone was so happy to see him. On one occasion when I took him back to his apartment, I can still hear Pat say, "I don't think you really know how much I love you!" It was rather odd, and it seemed that he had an urgency to tell me that.

A few days later I had the strangest dream I have ever had. I was standing outside looking up at the sky and it was the entire face of Jesus in black and white with outstretched arms. I remember telling a coworker that I had the strangest dream that I couldn't understand. A week later, I did understand.

*The book of life is brief, and once a page is read you can't undo it. Make each day count because tomorrow may never come, and one day there will be no chance to make peace or express your love. Write your own pages with happiness and confidence, and in the end, rest assured you made life count in a good way.

CHAPTER 29

Our Final Trip and a Lone Seagull

On the morning of May 15, 2017, I picked Pat up at the long-term care facility in Highlands, where he had resided for only three weeks, to start our long drive to Mayo Clinic in Jacksonville, Florida, for an appointment with his neurosurgeon. He was standing outside waiting with his little gray suitcase wearing a red windbreaker because it was rather chilly that morning. We started out with me driving, since I had convinced him years before that it was better if he did not drive again, and even though he didn't agree, he gave in. We were chatting all the way as I rested my hand on his knee. I was on the phone checking to see if a restaurant in Macon, Jeanene's, was open. It was one of our favorite places that served good old Southern cuisine. With Johnny cakes, turkey and the best dressing, fried pork chops, rutabagas, butter beans, field peas, and wonderful banana pudding, it was our go to place for lunch when living there.

Suddenly, I looked over, and "stuff" was coming out of Pat's mouth. I shockingly said, "Honey, are you nauseated?"

He couldn't speak, and I told him I would pull over and look for a towel. His last words were, "I'm sorry."

At that point, he collapsed and slumped over. I pulled to the side of the road, held him in my arms, and pushed the emergency button on my car. A man came on saying he had my location and would connect me with 911, and when she asked what the emergency was, I said I thought he had a heart attack but was still breathing. I often wondered if Pat heard me during all of this and what his thoughts were. Did he know he was dying? Did he hear me saying how much I loved him? Did he hear me praying to God to take him because I knew this was bad and he was unresponsive?

When the ambulance arrived, the driver was a jerk, and when I told him he was DNR (do not resuscitate), he asked if I had the papers. When I said that I didn't, he said he could not honor my word. I made him wait while I called Pat's doctor in Highlands, who came on the phone when I told the receptionist it was an emergency. He immediately told the driver Pat was DNR and I asked if he could email the form to me because I would need it at the ER.

I'll never forget the sound of the ambulance that day. After all, those sounds were always for someone else's tragedy, not mine. I followed it for the fifteen-minute drive to the Forsyth, Georgia, ER feeling scared and numb at the same time, and had to fill out paperwork before I could go back to see him.

They had cut off his beautiful plaid shirt of light blue and burgundy that brought out his rosy complexion in order to start an IV. Blood was drawn for labs, and he was still unresponsive. I held his hand, still wondering if he was aware of anything I said. I called Julie to tell her what had happened, and she immediately left to make the three-hour drive. The doctor came in and told me the heart enzymes were normal and I asked, "Well, what is this?"

He said they did not have an MRI machine but could do a CT scan and I insisted he do it. Meanwhile, to my surprise, my ex-husband, Lee, showed up in the room with us. Julie had called him and didn't want me to be alone. We hugged and he held me as I sobbed, knowing the end was near. It was surreal to have both of my husbands with me as one lay dying.

My doctor from Highlands called to check on us and told me, "Pat, for your sake and his, I hope he doesn't make it . . . it will be really bad!"

I thanked him for the call and waited for Pat's return from radiology. When he got back, his breathing was shallow, and the doctor came in to tell me it was a massive hemorrhagic stroke. A few many minutes later, he took his last breath, with me sobbing and holding his hand, telling him I loved him.

Unfortunately, Julie didn't arrive until fifteen minutes later and broke down in tears seeing this sweet man, who was such a big part of her life, had left this world. I don't even know how to express the emotions I felt. Numbness and auto-pilot took over my mind and body. I called his son and my brother to tell them. I could not stop sobbing and was incoherent. Once again, I looked at my surroundings in the small Forsyth, Georgia Hospital parking lot and saw people on their phones, talking and laughing, while my life was torn apart, once more.

Julie and I drove to Macon to get a hotel room since his body would be taken to the funeral home there. One of our dear friends, Phillip, drove from Soperton, Georgia, to comfort us. Julie and I held each other, trying to sleep, but sobbed uncontrollably. The visit to the funeral home was torture . . . this was supposed to happen to other people, not me. I could not allow myself physically or mentally see Pat to identify him, so Julie did it. He had wished to be cremated, and a week later I received a box filled with the remains of this gentle and loving man I shared the best years of my life with. I could not bear to open it. Later, his ashes would be scattered In Hilton Head, where our first trip together occurred, and Julie would take part of them to Grand Cayman Island where the three of us took many memorable scuba-diving trips.

I remember the drive home alone the following day sobbing and trying to convince myself I would wake up from this bad dream. When I walked into our condo, the realization hit me . . . I was alone for the first time in my life. Grief took over and for the first few weeks, I was so fatigued I couldn't get out of my chair. I didn't want to talk to people, and if I tried to go to the office and someone walked in, I broke down sobbing. It's a process that is personal to everyone, and there are no words to describe it or advice to give; you just live a day at a time. The clothes in his closet would remain there for a year because it would be too real to part with them.

A year went by before I could even hold the box with Pat's ashes in my hands; it seemed too real and painful. In December of 2018, I finally decided to make the trip to Hilton Head, South Carolina, alone to scatter the ashes in a place that connected us emotionally and intimately. I sat the wooden box, filled with the ashes of the man I loved so dearly, on the passenger seat, the same seat where he had collapsed on our last day together. I made the six-hour drive to Hilton Head to release him. I had reserved a room in the hotel, the old Mariner's Inn, now the Hilton, where we made our first trip together, on the same side of the building where we had stayed, not being sure of the room number. Memories rushed in as I arrived, and there was a chill in the air and a slight breeze from the ocean. That night, I slept with the box beside me as

I had once slept with him, awakening to a glorious sunrise and gentle sounds of the ocean.

I had coffee and said a prayer and then cradled the box in my arms, the same arms I cradled him in as he collapsed in the car on his last day on Earth and took the elevator downstairs. I wanted to do this at 11am on Sunday morning with a reverence we used to share in church. I finally gained the courage to open the box and was filled with sadness as I scattered a few ashes in the grass outside the room where we first shared intimacy as I was falling in love with this man, my husband to be. I continued down the path to the beach that we used to stroll together as we secured our beach chairs and basked in the sun on a lazy summer day.

I found a large stick and drew a huge heart in the semi-wet sand with only onlookers of seagulls and sandpipers. I opened the box once more and squeezed my hand into a fist, letting the ashes penetrate my fingernails. I scattered them in the heart of sand as only one seagull approached, standing close and watching curiously. I knew it was my Pat, witnessing this private ceremony in spirit. I said "I love you" as some of the ashes joined the wind above, slowly distributing them as they reached the ocean. At that moment, I remembered my dream a few days before Pat's death of the face of Jesus with arms outstretched, and knew he was looking down and smiling. He was home.

Finding true and mutual love has to be God's greatest gift. There are so many times that we think, "If I could just have enough money . . . if I could just get a better job . . . if my child could get into that college . . . if I could get a new car of my choice . . . if I could have more friends," on and on, but those things don't buy happiness and they don't last. It is the real love of oneself and our partner or spouse, along with faith in God to help guide us, that brings a joy that is everlasting. Grief of true love is worth the pain of never having loved at all.

CHAPTER 30

Cruise Ship and Mr. Magoo

I knew my first Christmas without Pat would be too difficult to face in similar surroundings, so my daughter, Julie, and I planned a cruise that would start in London, where my son lived and was a professor at the University, after achieving his PHD there years before. We arrived on December 22 jet lagged, but I was anxious to see Lee. We went to dinner, and it was so good to have both my kids together again. They filled my heart with gladness and for a short time took away my sadness.

The next day, Julie and I set out for a day of shopping. London was beautiful, filled with sparkling lights and festive green and red decorations overhead in the streets, and the store windows were glorious with silver and gold décor amid thousands of brilliant white lights. We were awestruck and proceeded to one of London's best department stores, Fenwick, that rivals Harrods. It opened its doors in 1891 and offers an array of services along with designer fashions and cosmetics. We chose to stay for high tea, London-style and it was fabulous! We then ventured out to find other stores and wound up with added weight for our luggage. It was unseasonably warm, so Julie and I ended the day sitting outside at a small café for light bites while surrounded by the Christmas lights and décor that filled the streets. It was the perfect end to a lovely day with a hint of magic in the air.

On Christmas Eve, we shopped a little more, rested a little, and met Lee for dinner at a local tapas place he suggested. It was crowded and filled with revelry, but we were seated in a room where we could actually hear each other. It was a great meal, filled with a lot of memories and discussion of past Christmases. Still, my mind would often drift to the realization that my sweet Pat would never share another Christmas tree, another beautifully wrapped gift, another trip to see festive lights or hear carolers or the excitement of Christmas morning anticipating a feast of traditional foods. I let the excitement of sailing to Spain and Portugal on Christmas afternoon ease the pain as best it could.

Christmas morning, we headed out by taxi to the port where the Cunard ship, Queen Mary 2, awaited. I always prefer an ocean liner because of the stabilizers that don't allow much motion. We checked in, walked the long ramp, and entered the lobby that exposed the grand staircase, filled with an enormous Christmas tree, decorated to the nines.

Shops filled the hallways and the mezzanine, as well. Shopping on a ship never really excited me or Pat, and we had cruised on seven different ships on our eleven voyages. We loved the gourmet food, entertainment, activities on board, excursions, various restaurants with theme dinners, wine-tasting events, movies with popcorn, and dancing to wonderful music. I even loved bingo, joined by hundreds of others, all feeling lucky that day. And I loved formal nights where you could dress up, feeling pretty and special—a throwback to a more glamorous past. British people have such a wonderful sense of humor, and the

Cunard became our favorite cruise line, even though the rooms weren't as grand as some of the other ships and the closet was "too tiny" for formal clothes.

We hurried to our rooms to unpack. We found the lounge and had a small plate and cappuccino, waiting for the dreaded mandatory drill wearing the prison orange-colored life jacket around our necks with tabs dangling until a crew member fixes it so you don't tumble overboard. I often wondered if you ever heard the call from the panic siren to evacuate the ship if you could or would remember where your lifeboat station was or if people would just panic and trample over each other. One thing was for sure: I didn't want to find out!

The first evening we met in the grand dining room and went to our assigned seats. The room was beautifully done and grand in every way. White tablecloths donned perfectly set tables with proper silverware, glassware, and ornate china that set expectations of a feast to come. You never know who will be seated with you, and it is always a pleasant surprise. There was an adorable couple about Julie's age from Australia, and they were charming and funny, and I loved their Aussie accents, and they loved my Southern drawl!

I glanced up to see an elderly gentleman steadying himself with a walker passing by us who seemed to know most of the waitstaff already. He sat at a table for two close to ours and I could see he wore a wedding band. His wife never showed up, and I thought maybe she was sick. We finished an incredible four course meal and headed to the theater for live entertainment. Again, I saw the same little man meander his way down front to a seat. He was still alone.

After a great musical presentation, we went to our rooms to get much-needed rest. Julie and I never share a room because

I stay up past her bedtime, and she arises before my eyes can possibly open. I went to the breakfast buffet, where you could find anything you could possibly want to eat, and being international cuisine, some I wanted to try. I sat sipping cappuccino by the window watching the water move past, putting us closer to Spain.

I made myself go to the gym most every day during our ten days of luxury living and over-indulging. The second night at dinner, once more the little old man shuffled to his table for two, alone again. Julie commented that we should ask him to join us since we had an extra chair and space. I mentioned it to the waiter, who went to ask the solo man, and immediately he stood up, turned around, smiled, and headed our way with no hesitation.

We all introduced ourselves and learned that his name was Ray and he lived right outside of London in Chesterfield. Surprisingly, he was living on a cruise ship for the rest of his life! We were intrigued, and his wit brought us many laughs.

During our week together, I would eventually learn the entire story. After dinner, we all headed to the theater again for the live show, with me sitting next to Ray. He told us there was big band music in the ballroom and he would love to have us join him. Julie opted out for sleep, but I was excited to go hear it, knowing how much my Pat would have enjoyed it, too.

I learned that Ray was eighty-four years old and, in my eyes, favored Mr. Magoo, the cartoon character. He had been a trumpet player and traveled to the states a few times with his band. His wife had died ten years earlier, but he still wore his wedding ring and still "talked" to her every night. He was estranged from his son, who he was in the insurance business with, and whose wife had neglected to let Ray's wife see their granddaughter, even knowing that she was dying. So, Ray decided to finish his last years aboard a cruise ship that provided all his needs. When one ship finished a cruise, he either continued on that one or disembarked to one of the others. Cunard has three ships: Queen Mary 2, Queen Elizabeth, and Queen Victoria. It was a sad but fascinating story, and for the next seven nights, Ray and I went to see the live entertainment show after dinner, followed by the sounds of the big band. You could feel the admiration he had for the trumpet players and memories must have resurfaced, reminding him of the days of old, when he took center stage.

He loved having a companion who appreciated music and he was quick to let the waiters, who knew him well over his previous four years as a passenger, that this "beautiful lady" dressed in lovely ball gowns was with him for the duration of the cruise. When the day to disembark came, Ray made a point to tell Julie and me how much he appreciated our companionship and how we had made this cruise his best ever. His eyes watered and we hugged, and I kissed him on the cheek. Little did he know how much he helped me though the first Christmas without the love of my life.

A few months later, I wanted to visit my son in London again and felt the need to prove to myself I could travel alone. I planned a trip on a Cunard ship, Queen Victoria, which would cross the Atlantic in a week, arriving in London. From there I would travel to Paris and Edinburgh by train to prove to myself that I could do it alone. Julie decided to email Ray to see if he was going to be on that ship at that date, and he was. I met him on the ship in New York and we had a lovely week of friendship and entertainment. I helped him pack the night before disembarkation because he was simply too tired to fool with it. He told me that I would never know how special our

time together made him feel and he would never forget that
week.

*Once again, the Holy Spirit sent me to Ray to bring joy back to
his life, and he to mine, for a short time anyway. You never know
what circumstances people are going through, and being kind is
a gift and the best gifts are tied with heartstrings.

CHAPTER 31

The Lemons Were Bitter...
But How Sweet the Lemonade

When my son, Lee III, was born, I literally prayed he would not be gay. The reason being I had seen the cruelty and hatred bestowed upon my gay brother, who was ten years older than I. He was beaten up by boys at school, and I remember my mother crying a lot and whispers were frequent so I could not hear. Back in the '60s and '70s, the life of a gay person was hell on Earth. The closet door stayed closed, and there had to be so much secrecy or you were dragged out of your car, beaten, spat on, and could lose your job for being the person you were born to be.

And yes, I say born to be, because I knew by the time he was three years old that my son was gay. I didn't cry because he was gay, I cried because I knew what he would face in the ugly world of haters who, in their world of religion, found this to be evil. Lee was a sweet child, and I could tell he was overly sensitive at a young age. He loved sitting in my closet with my necklaces on, putting my size six shoes on his tiny feet at ages three and four. I hoped it was just a phase, but deep down I knew it wasn't.

When he was around six, we wanted him to play tee ball like the other boys in the neighborhood and hoped to get him into sports. He hated it, and even though he was a big boy for his age, he wasn't very good at it. This prompted him to say "no" to little league, which the other boys were into. I think this was hard on his dad, who was into sports and had many friends at the University of Georgia, who were great football players and who had high hopes for his namesake. When we convinced Lee to try miniature football, he came home and asked, "Why do I want to run across a field with a ball, with boys chasing me to knock me down and hurt me?"

He was smarter than most at that age, and we didn't pursue sports for him after that intelligent assessment of football.

When Lee was in first grade, we received a letter from his teacher stating she felt he was a gifted child, and we didn't really know what that meant. I just thought he was quicker to read than other students, but the teacher explained that gifted kids excelled and were quick to get bored easily and it was not always a good thing. Luckily, the grammar school in our neighborhood had a gifted program for these kids. Julie would also enter the program two years later. They were taught on a different level, with creative ideas and activities that stimulated their thought processes.

There was also a class for handicapped children in the school and the gifted kids intermingled with them on occasion, even learning to play chess. They also learned to appreciate kids with disabilities and not make fun of them, as many other kids did. Lee loved to play with our neighbor's daughter, Lori Ann, who lived right next door. Another neighbor had a son, Todd, who was big into playing sports, but his mother was kind enough to invite Lee over for meals, movies, or sleepovers, so there were a few boys he befriended.

We were avid churchgoers and wanted to make sure Lee and Julie were Christians, so whenever the church doors opened, we were usually there. We were always good friends with the associate pastors since they were usually close to our ages. There was one in particular who we were friends with, and he and his wife and their little boy would share meals or church trips or other activities together with us. At about the same time as my divorce, two of my other girlfriends had gotten divorced, both having loser husbands who spent little or no time with their sons. Once I was divorced, this pastor started spending more and more time with the boys, having sleepovers, and renting movies, as DVDs were just becoming available. We, the mothers, were thrilled that they had a male figure in their lives who wanted to spend time with them. I should have seen the red flag, but I trusted this person and it never occurred to me he was a pedophile who preyed on boys. I didn't know this until many years later when I asked Lee why he never wanted to go to the pastor's house anymore and he answered with dead silence. When he told me, my heart sank and I sobbed, feeling that I had failed to protect my son. He assured me that nothing happened after pushing the minister away and telling him to get his hands off him! This is the same pastor I trusted all those years and had chosen to marry Pat and me. I felt so betrayed.

Many years later this minister would be arrested, but I wonder how many boys he molested, ruining their lives. One boy we knew killed himself and I'll always wonder if that was why. Evil does exist, even in God's name. The clergy have a role in saving our souls . . . not scarring our minds. Tread softly but know this was an exception to God's rule and his role.

CHAPTER 32

The One Question You Never Want to Be Asked, But I Had the Answer

Her name was Cheryl. She was a widow from my hometown of Macon, but she was a few years older than me. Even though we attended the same high school, she had already graduated when I started there, so I never knew her but remembered her name. She was a debutante, beauty queen, and from a prominent family, so all the things I wasn't. So, it's fascinating that she and I both wound up in Highlands and shared her final years together. Honestly, I don't remember exactly how we met. At some function, I suppose.

When we finally connected and started going out, her sense of humor kept me laughing and she adored my sweet husband Pat, who was still living at that time. She would always pucker up and he would pucker up but never touch lips. We would all laugh. There were a few other girls we would go to dinner with, but Cheryl didn't like one of them, so she stopped going with us. She said this person was not nice and made her feel uncomfortable. Later, I learned she was right, and I learned the hard way. I was betrayed and hurt deeply by that "friend."

I remember during a snowstorm, Cheryl didn't have a good driveway for wheels on the snow, so when I called to check on her, she said she could use a few things from our local grocery store, Bryson's, and gave me a short list that also included Chardonnay and a bottle of vodka. The liquor store was nearby also, so I obliged. I didn't realize at the time the hint I was given.

She had an old oil furnace that was gigantic and groaned like a moose caught in barbed wire. Cheryl named her Big Bertha. Sometimes she wouldn't fire up and it would literally be freezing in her house in the winter. I would offer to bring her to our house, but she always refused. She became more and more reclusive. She was my Facebook friend and her wit delighted me and so many of her friends.

She started to post about vertigo, and I would text that she should see a doctor. She refused, until one evening in October of 2017, she started hemorrhaging and called 911. The house design was odd in that the great room was downstairs and she had to climb significant stairs to get to her front door. There was no way she could do that, so the EMTs had to break it down. She was sent to our local emergency room, but when they saw she was critical they rushed her to a larger hospital in Asheville, North Carolina. After the examination, the doctor called in the family and said he did not expect her to survive since her hemoglobin was so low and her liver was destroyed by cirrhosis. She had two daughters and a son who were rushing to see her. Her life was spared for whatever reason, and a decision had to be made: where should she go? The doctor said the prognosis was not good and he couldn't say how long she might survive.

Her daughter found a very nice, assisted living facility in Lawrenceville, Georgia. When Cheryl was able to share again on Facebook, I learned where she was. I texted her and told her

I would come and visit, and I did. I drove up to a lovely building and was a little nervous as to how she would look and how I would react. I walked inside to the receptionist's desk, who had been alerted that Cheryl had a visitor coming. The place reminded me of the facility my dear Pat was in for a few months prior to his death. There were people in wheelchairs who rolled past or sat by the window for the comfort of the rays of the sun, reminding them of times when they could frolic and play, perhaps at the seashore or perhaps in their own yard as they planted a garden or watched grandchildren play. I had empathy for them, knowing this was their final home and not by choice.

I was shown the way to Cheryl's room and when she opened the door, we hugged like family. She was thinner and her eyes were not as bright as they once were. She still smiled and was the same old Cheryl with humor despite it all. The room was small with a loveseat, chair, and a television always on Fox News. The bathroom had a shower that later became filled with clothes and paraphernalia. The bed was queen sized, the dresser adequate, and the closet small. This was her home and her lifeline now. I visited her as often as I could and got to know so much about her life that many had never known.

Looking back and after talking with one of her daughters, it seems Cheryl probably needed therapy early in life and her marriage was not a happy one, according to Cheryl although she loved her husband dearly. The role of motherhood was difficult for her, and her children didn't receive the devotion and love needed from a mother. I don't think Cheryl was capable of giving it. She never really had a good relationship with her children or any family members. I was sad to learn this for all involved.

Cheryl decided to sell the house in Highlands, I saw it for the first time. I was alone, and when I entered, I was shocked at the condition of the home. Downstairs, blood had dried, and I could see the chair that was her respite from the society she once knew. The house was in disarray and hadn't been cleaned in months, maybe years. There had been a water leak in the kitchen and mold was growing. There were antiques and silver amidst the mess, and I thought there must have been some happiness there when her older husband was living. But at some point, everything changed.

One daughter told me that when she and her husband and kids would visit Highlands, they weren't allowed to come to Cheryl's house. They stayed in a hotel and met Cheryl at the restaurant of wherever their destination for the day was. I then came to realize that Cheryl drank a lot at home and that became her escape from mistakes she made and never had the courage to face or try to correct.

Cheryl's health deteriorated and the cirrhosis turned into liver cancer and lymphoma. She received blood transfusions every Monday and her reactions to the chemo were severe. I continued to make the two-hour trip to visit as often as my time allowed, and each time her weight loss was disturbing. We would sit in the private alcove and share lunch as the residents wheeled by, always speaking to Cheryl. She would introduce me, and on their departure, fill me in on their stories. I would fill her in on stories from Highlands, the good and the bad. She missed it terribly, along with any normalcy of life. Her sweet dog, Maggie, had been Cheryl's companion and moved into the facility with her. The little bed reeked but was filled with loving memories. She died about a year into Cheryl's three long, hellish years in this facility. Cheryl and I cried together.

My final visit was on Valentine's Day, 2022. I felt the urge to make the drive and took a dozen red roses to Cheryl. She was thrilled but looked worse than I had ever seen her. We chatted and hugged tight, allowing me to feel her extended ribs. Her hair was thin, and her teeth darkened. We chatted for a while about life and world politics, and she tried to make it as upbeat as possible, but I sensed a change and words left unspoken. I remember when I left, she walked right outside the main door to wave goodbye, and I knew that was the last time I would see her.

I received a text from Cheryl early one morning in February of 2022. She said she really needed to talk with me, and I told her to call. She always had trouble getting her phone to work there, but we connected. She started off by saying, "Pat, you are the only one that will be honest with me. I just don't know what to do. I spend my days getting transfusions now and it takes six hours of just sitting there."

The gist of the conversation was her asking if she should keep going or let go. I had never had anyone ask if they should let their life end before. But from somewhere deep within me, the response came. When I asked her what she looked forward to each day, she replied, "The only thing I have now is pain."

I replied, "Cheryl, you know I can't make that decision for you. But I would make peace with my children and God and then you are ready to stop enduring pain."

She said, "I love you, Pat."

I replied, "I love you, Cheryl."

She did what I subliminally relayed and stopped the transfusions and allowed the natural process to occur, ending her life on March 2, 2022. Our last texts were on February 22, 2022, when she sent a picture of us with her holding the roses. We both ended the text expressing our love for each other.

I know God knew Cheryl needed a genuine friend, and I knew she needed a nudge and permission to let go. The Holy Spirit once more had sent me on a mission. Rest in peace, Cheryl. You brought joy and laughter to so many. I'm glad you entered my life.

CHAPTER 33

Grief Comes in All Sizes...
Not One Size Fits All

These are my personal reflections on grief I have experienced. How do you describe grief? How do you cope with it? Does it ever end? Is there a formula to deal with it and move on? Does it ever go away? There are so many questions regarding grief, and once we are faced with it personally, we realize there are no simple answers. It is a journey through the tangled wilderness of human emotions, where each path is unique, and no destination guarantees closure.

I have dealt with grief in the loss of my dad, my mother, and my husband, followed a year later by the death of my dear brother. Each one happened at a different stage in my life and left its indelible mark on my soul and a void in my heart as I experienced each one in different ways.

I was thirty years old when my dad died, and I was holding his hand as he left this world. I can still feel the numbness that flowed through my body. We were alone in his hospital room as his battle with pancreatic cancer came to an end. The suffering he endured for six months, leaving his body weight to be a mere sixty-eight pounds of bones covered slightly with flesh, was cause to welcome the arms of death that ended his life.

This was my first experience with mortality, and I was forced to accept that death is real; it lurks behind closed passageways and picks and chooses its next victim and then reaches out and squeezes the last breath of life from them. It brings you to your core existence until you finally beg to be taken rather than live in pain or have a machine continue your miserable existence.

In my dad's case, I experienced the realization of death of a family member for the first time. The sense of loss was followed by anger that cancer was allowed to destroy this man who gave me life, who made me laugh, who held my hand as a little girl offering security in an uncertain world, who took me fishing, who adored my two small children as their grandfather, who was gentle and had a good soul. It was overwhelming and prompted me to see what really matters in life. It was a turning point, and I knew my marriage was failing and it needed to end allowing myself, my husband, and my two young children to move on in hopes of a better life for all.

My mother's diagnosis of lung cancer twenty-three years later shook my world once more. She was strong and never asked for help from anyone, having been raised by various family members and never knowing the bond a child and mother normally have. Her dad left before she was born, never to be seen again. Poverty played a major role in her life, and she was determined to make a better life for her children. In that regard she succeeded, although it was riddled with disappointments with my dad's drinking problem. She endured and we all made the most of it.

As far as her cancer, she didn't suffer as much as my dad had, and in the end, pneumonia filled her lungs as she struggled to breathe, asking me to help her on her deathbed. I begged her to let go, knowing she was frightened and the cancer that was growing would cause more suffering. She finally gave in, and I held her hand as she was taken from me. Once more numbness filled my body, but I also experienced denial when my brother, sister, and I went to dinner as if this horrible event hadn't just happened. Because Pat and I were living in Highlands and Mama was living in Macon, I think the distance helped because I didn't see her often. In my mind she was still there, until I would go to the phone to call her and was brought to my knees knowing she was gone.

When my sweet Pat was first diagnosed with hydrocephalus after he started being forgetful and his gait changed, I felt the same numbness I had experienced with the previous deaths, even though he would live six more years. This disease causes a small amount of spinal fluid to be released into the brain, creating confusion and memory loss that can mimic dementia in many ways. The head of neurology at Mayo Clinic determined that surgery to reroute the fluid would more than likely result in a stroke, and he didn't recommend it. He said the process would be slow and to go and enjoy our time together.

This was when I learned that grieving is not just for the physical death of a person, but also the mental death of someone. I was living with this man I knew so well but was now a stranger in many ways. I woke up every day to the unknown of what would happen next; I had no control of the mental decline of this man I loved deeply but who was slowly becoming someone I didn't know. I wanted to "fix" it and became angry inside when he didn't respond the way he used to with normal day to day things. I missed the person I laughed with, had great conversations with, traveled with, was passionate with, and made plans for the future with.

This type of grief is very different from that of death. I became depressed and tried to work harder so I didn't have to think. As the years passed, I was living with a man who looked just like my husband who was the love of my life but was now someone I did not know. He was never mean though, and that was a blessing. I often think of the day I realized that mental death had occurred and seeing him every day was a reminder of my loss. It was emotionally tortuous to accept that my dear husband as I knew him no longer existed. I'm sure many of you have experienced this with someone in your family who has/had Alzheimer's or dementia and they have no memories of you as you gaze into a blank face.

On our last visit to see the neurologist at Mayo Clinic, we were told that we were now dealing with the other side of the brain, and when I asked if the doctor meant Alzheimer's, my world was rocked once more when he said, "Yes."

Pat didn't comprehend what he said, but as I walked down the hall to my doctor's appointment and entered a waiting room of people who glanced as I sobbed uncontrollably until a nurse took me to the back immediately, trying to console me. There are just no words to describe this type of grief and fear of the unknown you are facing. Fear is ever-present and creates an array of emotions you haven't experienced before.

I think post-traumatic stress disorder plays a part in this role of cruelty in life. It is defined as a condition of persistent mental and emotional stress occurring because of severe psychological shock. Diagnosis of a terminal illness, whether mental or physical, knowing you are facing loss of a loved one can easily trigger this and we are never quite the same person we were before.

On the morning of May 15, 2017, while I was driving Pat to Mayo for an evaluation, he collapsed in the car, and when I pulled over on the side of the road on Interstate 75, I just held him, telling him how much I loved him while asking God to please take him. The massive hemorrhagic stroke would have left him brain dead, and four hours later God answered my prayer. My grief became different, as I felt I was given a blessing that he would no longer have to endure this dreaded disease with the loss of all dignity that could linger for years. It didn't stop the void I felt then and still feel, but I know it was the better of our two choices.

A year later I would face death and grief with the loss of my brother, who had always been there when I needed him. The role reversed when he was suffering with non-alcoholic cirrhosis of his liver. He was a savior of stray animals and even displaced people in need. He struggled physically for the last two years of his life and hemorrhaged several times as his liver tried to process food but was blocked by scarring. He was single and very independent and would struggle to drive himself to the hospital.

As he became weaker and no longer had the strength to get out of bed, I drove to Macon from Highlands to take him to the hospital in Atlanta. I held back my tears as I saw this sweet man struggle to walk to my car as he said goodbye to the dogs he had rescued. This was the man who made me laugh with his quick wit, who helped anyone in need, and who was my rock when Pat died; now I had to be his. Seeing him give in to death wrenched my heart as I watched him struggle to the end as I held his hand as his body finally had enough and shook with a seizure as if to say, "I'm done!"

The numbness came once more, and as I left the room and found the nurse at her computer to alert her, I saw the words "This eighty-year-old man with AIDS," my heart sank knowing the medications he took for many years had destroyed his liver.

He and I had never discussed him being gay, and my sadness was in part the cruelty of life and not being accepted for just being who he was, and he was a gentle and kind soul and a great man.

*You can see from my four experiences of death that grief has no pattern or template, and each situation affected me in different ways. With each passing, a strength was pulled from some unknown place, allowing me to wake up each day and move forward. It has been six years since the death of my sweet husband and sometimes I can talk about him without tears and other times the tears still flow. There is no rhyme or reason to the emotions that grief conjures up. People depend on us to keep going, and one day they will grieve our loss as we take our last breath.

CHAPTER 34

Conclusions and Illusions

I have learned that whether you had a bad childhood, an alcoholic parent, little money, suffered abuse, had friends betray you, a husband who deceived and hurt you, or are just plain miserable with choices you have made, you can still survive and thrive. Look at who YOU are . . . not who THEY are. I've often seen women who got divorced and then married the same type of man, resulting in the same pattern of behavior. They mistakenly believe they deserve to be treated that way because it's all they know. It is hard to analyze oneself, and I do believe therapy is beneficial.

Lately, I have become intrigued with hypnotherapy which resets the thoughts in your conscious mind by engaging the subconscious mind to change the way you feel and replace negative thoughts with positive feelings. It is an amazing process, and I just became certified to help others with issues that hold them back from ever reaching their full potential. Do surround yourself with good people who are happy with themselves, not those who are miserable and bring you down. That only creates a sounding board for pity and nothing good comes from it.

*In summary, being stuck is a state of mind, and once you take charge of your own life and let go of your fear, you can move on and explore what really makes you happy. Love is the greatest gift of all but it's not possible to share until you learn to love yourself first. Putting that responsibility on another is more than they can handle, and sooner or later they will walk away, leaving you to start the process again. Having built your foundation on faith by the world's greatest architect, God, the world's greatest carpenter, Jesus Christ, and prayer and daily guidance from the Holy Spirit, you can weather any storms that come your way and withstand grief and pain knowing the Holy Trinity is there to lift you up if you simply ask and BELIEVE.

You will see when reading my book that I had enormous hurdles and at times felt like quitting. But quitters never get to the other side, where opportunity awaits, where hope prevails, and where love is waiting.

Epilogue

I have learned that gratitude is a force that enriches our lives in so many ways. It shifts our focus from what we lack to what we have, resulting in contentment and inner peace. By appreciating the blessings, big or small, we cultivate a positive outlook, reducing stress and enhancing overall well-being. Gratitude also strengthens relationships, as expressing thanks deepens our connections. It results in kindness and empathy, making the world a better place. Embracing gratitude is a pathway to a more fulfilling life. I am so grateful for having had the strength to jump every hurdle resulting in confidence, achievements, and inner peace.

I have learned that confidence is the key to unlocking one's full potential and transforming their life. When we believe in ourselves and our abilities, we approach challenges with resilience and enthusiasm. Confidence fosters a positive self-image, attracting opportunities and enabling us to take risks. Walking into a room with successful people, holding my head high, and sometimes "winging it" has led others to believe in me. Perception is an important part of success. If you look the part and act the part (even though you may be unsure of just what the part is), others will believe in your ability to accomplish your goals. There have been times when I did "fake it 'til I made it," and with positive results. Confidence improves communication, enhances relationships, and bolsters leadership qualities. Moreover, confidence breeds a sense of empowerment and self-worth, leading to personal growth and success. It's the catalyst for pursuing dreams, jumping hurdles, and ultimately creating a life filled with purpose and achievement.

I have learned that the concept of persistence is a powerful drive of achievement and personal growth. It embodies the tenacity to pursue our goals despite challenges and setbacks. It's the unwavering belief that with continuous effort and determination, success is attainable. I know I come across as too strong, too outspoken, and have been called the "B word" because I stand up for what I believe in. Persistence fuels resilience, teaching us valuable lessons through failures and setbacks. It separates the dreamers from the achievers, propelling individuals to jump hurdles, reach their potential, and turn aspirations into reality. In essence, persistence is the fuel that powers the journey to success.

I have learned that we all have angelic potential to help others on this Earth: it's not by invitation only. So many times, and when I least expect it the number 333 appears, and I know this is another sign of an angelic aura. Some only tap into the beginning stage of angelic endearment while others soar to heights unknown, changing other's lives. You can choose your wing size . . . one size does not fit all.

I have learned that the best gifts in life are tied with heartstrings.

Wishing you a happy and fulfilled life from this day forward.

Pat Allen

I may be contacted at: therealpatallen@gmail.com or PO BOX 809, Highlands, North Carolina 28741

I am available for speaking engagements.

Disclaimer: Names have been changed or omitted to protect privacy of the individual or businesses involved. Situations are truthful to the author's recollection as described herein.

No harm is intended to any individual or family member. The book is intended to be inspiration and the situations incurred are relevant to the story.

Favorites from Whisk Upon a Star from our Morning Star Inn

MORNING STAR GRANOLA

1 1/2 cups old fashioned oats 1/2 cup shredded coconut 1/2 teaspoon cinnamon
2 tablespoons butter, melted.
1/2 teaspoon vanilla
1/8 cup honey
1/2 cup chopped nuts (any kind) 1/2 cup raisins or dried fruit.

Mix oats, coconut, and cinnamon in an ungreased baking dish or sheet pan. Combine butter, vanilla, honey, and nuts. Pour over dry ingredients and mix. Bake at 350 degrees for 15 to 20 minutes, stirring every 5 to 10 minutes. Remove when brown and add raisins or dried fruit. May be doubled.

Serve with diced apples and yogurt (vanilla or plain) on top.

Note: This is probably the most requested recipe by our guests. It was also requested by Bon Appetit Magazine and won 1st place as the best B & B granola in the country by the National Baking Association!

PADDY'S GRITS

4 cups water
1 teaspoon salt
1 cup quick cooking grits
8 slices American cheese
1/2 teaspoon garlic powder 3 to 4 dashes Tabasco

Bring salted water to a boil. Stir in grits, reduce heat, and cook for 5 minutes or until grits begin to thicken, add cheese, one slice at a time, stirring well. Add garlic powder and Tabasco. Adjust seasonings as necessary.

Note: Patrick's own recipe and always loved by our guests ... even Yankees!

Southwestern Eggs

10 eggs
1 stick butter
1/2 cup flour
1 teaspoon baking powder 2 cups cottage cheese
2 (4-ounce) cans diced green chiles,
drained
1 teaspoon salt
1 pound Monterey jack cheese,
shredded

Preheat oven to 350 degrees. Whisk eggs in large bowl. Whisk in butter, flour, baking powder, cottage cheese, chilies, and salt. Fold in Monterey Jack cheese. Bake in 9 x 13-inch glass dish sprayed with non- stick cooking spray for 40 to 45 minutes.

Note: *This is the first recipe we served our guests upon opening the inn, everyone loves this! Can top with salsa and sour cream- I like it plain.*

YUM YUM Cornbread

1 cup self-rising cornmeal
1 teaspoon salt
Pinch of baking soda
2 eggs, beaten.
1 small can cream corn
1 small carton sour cream
½ cup cooking oil

Spray baking dish with non-stick cooking spray. Preheat oven to 350 degrees. Combine corn meal, salt, baking soda, eggs, corn, sour cream, and oil. Stir just until blended. Pour into baking dish and bake for 45-50 minutes until golden brown.

Note: *This is my favorite cornbread and so easy!*

About the Author

PAT ALLEN, a multifaceted individual, relocated to Highlands, NC over two decades ago, marking the beginning of a new chapter in her illustrious career. This move led to the establishment of the Morning Star Inn, a reputable Bed and Breakfast Inn complemented by a cooking school. A testament to her achievements, Southern Living Magazine recognized her establishment as one of their favorites. The inn ran for an impressive seven years under Pat's expert guidance.

Her flair for design, stemming from her stint as a decorator in Macon, GA, combined with a two-year culinary training, played pivotal roles in the success of her ventures. Her journey through the culinary world was further enriched as she donned the hat of a food critic and shared kitchen space with renowned celebrity chefs. This culinary voyage culminated in the publication of two cookbooks penned by Pat herself: "Whisk upon a Star" and "Mouth of the South."

The name 'Morning Star Inn' was inspired by a church hymn, showcasing Pat's profound connection to her spiritual side. This venture wasn't just business for her. She felt a deep-rooted calling to initiate it. As time went on, it became evident that the inn served as a sanctuary for many of her guests. They opened up to Pat about their personal tragedies, solidifying her belief that this path was destined for her.

In her personal life, Pat shared a wonderful marriage of thirty-three years with her husband, Dr. Pat Allen - a retired oral surgeon hailing from Jackson, Mississippi, who boasts an impressive background as a former Mayo Clinic fellow. He passed away six years ago prompting her into the hurdle of grief.

But Pat's expertise isn't limited to inns and cookery. With a keen eye for homes and a knack for decorating, she transitioned smoothly into a lucrative career in real estate. After serving as the Broker-in-Charge at a local firm in Highlands, NC for seven years, and consistently outshining her peers, Pat ventured on to establish her own firm, Pat Allen Realty Group. Her accolades in real estate are numerous - from being a certified luxury home marketing specialist in the region to being a proud member of both the Million Dollar Guild and the Institute for Luxury Homes. Her unparalleled efforts in the field led her to be crowned The Best Realtor (R) in Highlands by The Highlander's readership. Her success led to a merger with Allen Tate Realtors based in Charlotte, North Carolina, the largest and most successful independent real estate firm in the country and proud members of Leading Real Estate Companies of the World and Luxury Portfolio. She continues to excel in Highlands, North Carolina.

Licensed in both NC & GA, Pat's success is a reflection of her relentless hard work, unwavering dedication to her clientele, and her exceptional negotiating and marketing skills.

"The most beautiful people we have known are those who have known defeat, known suffering, known struggle, known loss, and have found their way out of the depths. These persons have an appreciation, a sensitivity, and an understanding of life that fills them with compassion, gentleness, and a deep loving concern. Beautiful people do not just happen."

Elisabeth Kubler-Ross

Made in the USA
Columbia, SC
01 May 2024

35124634R00100